Running a Flat
Management Com

Running a Flat Management Company

Third Edition

Nigel G. Cox MA (HONS) OXON
Solicitor, Alsters & Cox, Bath

JORDANS

2000

Published by
Jordan Publishing Limited
21 St Thomas Street
Bristol BS1 6JS

British Library Cataloguing-in-Publication Data

A catalogue record for this book is available from the British Library.

ISBN 0 85308 604 4

Typeset by Mendip Communications Ltd, Frome, Somerset
Printed by MPG Books Ltd, Bodmin, Cornwall

Preface

It is now some ten years since I was first approached to write a book about the relatively unfashionable topic of management of blocks of flats by their owners. At the time, I had no idea just how many people would find the book useful. With this third edition, I have the opportunity of reviewing the changes which occurred during the period. There is no doubt that a lot has happened in the world of flat management, and most of it for the better. Largely due to public pressures, the law has undergone many significant changes, particularly with the enfranchisement legislation enacted in 1993 and subsequent amendments. At the time of writing, consultation is well underway on further legislation. There is no doubt that the rights of flat-owners have improved and the ability to take control of the landlord role is a highly valued prize in the search by flat-owners to provide for good management of their properties.

The fundamental problem of management is entrusting that management to a group of lay residents, who, understandably, find it difficult to come to grips with the legal requirements imposed upon them. Solicitors and accountants may frequently be called in to assist in running the management company's affairs which can be expensive and is often unnecessary, but there remain a variety of problems to deal with. Sometimes, it is the apparently simple task of setting up such a company but, more often, it is to put right a lengthy history of errors in filing documents, failed management, inter-flat squabbles or a selection of other equally frustrating problems.

Many of these problems are born out of a misunderstanding by the officers of the management company of the essential requirements of running their company. Such misunderstandings are, perhaps, to be expected. Very often the directors and the company secretary of a flat management company are men or women who have had the responsibility of looking after the administration of their building thrust upon them, whether by accident or design, or simply because someone had to do it. Often such companies neither wish nor can afford to employ professionals to service their company on a daily basis and it is for these people that this book has been written.

Preface

This book is not an academic study of the world of the management company, or intended to equip a lay person to carry out the more complex areas of procedure in the life of a management company. It is designed to be an accessible guide for the individual or group of individuals coming to the problem of flat ownership and block management for the first time. In areas such as accounting, enfranchisement and many other areas, there remains no substitute for professional advice. What this book attempts to do, as simply as possible, is to provide an outline guide for the people running their own flat management company of what to do, when to do it, and how to cope when things go wrong. Thus armed with a basic knowledge of procedure, and a modicum of common sense, the officers of a flat management company (its directors and company secretary) will be better able to perform their duties and obligations with confidence and in a cost-effective way. It will also result in a deeper understanding of those tasks which are better left to the professional adviser (the solicitor, the accountant or the surveyor) so that approaches to such advisers are informed and well prepared, and thus ensure a more cost-effective professional service from advisers.

Each chapter addresses a specific area of interest, and is split into sections, providing the reader with the opportunity to dip into its contents to find answers to specific problems which arise during the life of a flat management company.

Where appropriate, reference is made to the forms required under current legislation to be filed at Companies House and identifies those areas where the officers are best advised to obtain professional assistance. Check-lists are provided to guide the company's officers through meetings and other procedures.

An invaluable feature of this book is its star-rating system which indicates the degree of need to take professional advice. One star means advice is desirable; two stars means it is strongly recommended; and three stars means it is crucial. Where a topic is given a no-star rating, the task may usually be undertaken without professional advice – but remember, when in doubt, ask an expert.

Of the many ways to run a management company, the limited company still remains the major vehicle although other structures are referred to in the book. With the threat of penalties for directors of limited companies who fail to comply with certain formal requirements, other methods of management may arise in the future. Where applicable, the text of this book incorporates all recent legislation, but the area of leasehold reform is still a topic of considerable interest and further developments can be expected in the future. This book addresses the problems of flat management from the point of view primarily of the limited company since it is this structure with which the flat-owner will normally be familiar and in connection with which he or she will have to cope.

Essentially, the requirements of running a flat management company are like those of any other company and, once the habit of organisation has been grasped, it is very often a question of following a set of standard procedures. If these are followed, then at least the likelihood of the company being struck off the register, and the expensive implications of such an event occurring, may be avoided. The problem of running the company is often the fact that in any block of flats there is likely to be a regular turnover of owners resulting in no one person ever being in a position for long enough to provide continuity of management from year to year.

The other problems likely to be encountered relate to the interrelationship between individual flat-owners. As an officer of the company, the company secretary or a director, may well find him- or herself acting as referee in disputes, or having to answer difficult questions on maintenance charges at the annual general meeting. He or she becomes a personal target for disgruntled flat-owners.

At the very worst, it may be his or her task to rescue the company after it has been badly neglected by a predecessor. Such neglect is fairly common and, in certain circumstances, may even require the resurrection of the company after it has been struck off the register.

I am very grateful to Cecile Gillard of Jordans Ltd for providing the original forms in Appendix 1 and for the useful summary of the statutory requirements in relation to company stationery in Chapter 10. More generally, I am indebted to all those clients whose trials and tribulations prompted me to write this guide in the first place and to the many others who, since the first edition was published, have shared further experiences enabling me to elaborate in certain areas. The law is stated as at January 2000.

NIGEL G. COX

Contents

hapter **One**
Methods of Flat Management

Why have a management structure?

Flat-owners are a diverse group of people whose one common feature is that they share a building which is separated into individually owned and occupied units. Each unit relies on all the others for support and protection. They are interdependent and, without being enveloped in an integrated structure, each unit would soon become impossible to manage and, perhaps, in the worst case, unsaleable. Every flat-owner should ensure that a proper structure is in place which provides rules for enforcing obligations between flat-owners, between flat-owners and the management company, and for the way the building as a whole is maintained and insured.

Most freehold property owners never have to address these issues because they are absolute owners of all parts of their property. Flat-owners are always presented with more complex situations arising from the nature of their ownership because they collectively share certain parts of the property and certain obligations. Only in the case of a building consisting of two flats is the problem unlikely to be present. In such cases, mutual convenants usually regulate quite adequately the interrelationship of the two flat-owners, and circumstance and economics would not justify any other formal structure.

In larger blocks of flats, a structure needs to be set up, preferably at the outset, to regulate affairs. The larger the block or development, the more complex the management affairs are likely to become. In the very largest developments, the responsibility for management may well remain with the original freeholder or its managing agents since the economies of scale justify a continuing involvement by the freehold owner and the revenue from rent is worth retaining. Often, the value of the building renders enfranchisement unfeasible (see p 31). It is in medium-sized blocks that the flat-owners may wish the control of management to be transferred from the freeholder to themselves.

The need for a formal and regulated structure between flat-owners may not always seem obvious to the flat-owners themselves or to a landlord who still owns or has developed the property. It is not unknown to find situations where flat-owners have carried on running their building in the absence of any proper management from the existing owner, and subsequently discovered that the owner, being a limited company, has gone into liquidation and that the building has not been insured for many years, with resulting disastrous and expensive consequences if any damage occurred during the uninsured period.

What is the purpose of a management company?

Under the terms of flat leases, the flat-owner will have entered into covenants with the landlord which are necessary for the efficient running of the block. These covenants are obligations which are contractually binding on the flat-owner personally. The usual provisions will relate to the payment of rent, insurance premiums and service charges. In addition, there will be covenants restricting or regulating the way in which each flat-owner will behave in relation to neighbours, or how he or she uses the property.

Without some separately identifiable body enforcing the covenants and collecting monies due under the terms of a lease, management of the building would break down. In addition, management of common parts, the provision of services to the flat-owners, collection of rents and day-to-day problems will go unattended. Proper management is, therefore, not only advisable but essential.

Different forms of management

SIMPLEST MANAGEMENT – 'CRISS-CROSS'

The simplest form of management structure is demonstrated by the case of a building which is split into two flats. Each flat-owner shares the responsibility of looking after the property equally. No other management structure is necessary. The freehold of the property may be vested in one or other of the flat-owners, or each may own the other's freehold title (commonly known as a 'criss-cross lease'). It is not usually necessary to use any form of company structure in such cases, although sometimes the requirements of lending institutions may make it advisable, even in such circumstances.

THE DEVELOPER AS MANAGER

The original owner (often a developer or builder), or any other person or company who subsequently acquires that owner's interest, may choose to retain the freehold and, as landlord, assume responsibility for management, either directly or through managing agents. As explained before, this is often of interest to a landlord where the size of the development or building justifies the retention of its interest in the property, and management is similar to where a property is let for commercial reasons as an investment property, where the rents are set at commercial levels to justify the value of the investment. An owner in this situation may be vulnerable to enfranchisement by the flat-owners.

Acquisition through statute/ enfranchisement

RIGHTS OF FIRST REFUSAL

In 1987, for the first time, tenants of blocks of flats obtained rights to acquire their building from a landlord. Under the Landlord and Tenant Act 1987, provisions were enacted to give qualifying tenants the right to first refusal to acquire their freehold where the landlord wished to sell. Additional provisions were included to allow tenants greater say in management where a landlord carried out his obligations inadequately. Since landlords, willing to dispose of their freehold interest, often approach their tenants in any event, these provisions have not made a great impact on the method of acquisition. In addition, the provisions were difficult to enforce, but landlords now commit a criminal offence if they fail to comply with the provisions as to first refusal.

COMPULSORY ENFRANCHISEMENT

Since the introduction in 1993 of the statutory right to enfranchise, or put more simply the giving to flat-owners of the legal right to force a landlord to sell its freehold to the collective flat-owners, the world of flat management has been slowly changing. No longer are flat-owners forced to accept inadequate or exploitative management by non-resident owners. Providing they are eligible, they can set up their own nominee company to acquire and then run block management. The number of groups enfranchising is growing quite fast and private landlords, aware of the power now wielded by flat-owners, are in many cases modifying the way in which they approach management.

Both the above provisions are dealt with in Chapter 3.

RESIDENTS' ASSOCIATIONS

A residents' association must be contrasted with a formally constituted and incorporated management company. It is normally an ad hoc grouping of flat-owners brought together to exert moral pressure upon a landlord. However, it must be stressed that such an association will have no legal status (although it may become a recognised resident's association) and a landlord in such cases will not be obliged either himself or through his managing agents to consult such a body. If such an association has no legal right of representation on behalf of the flat-owners, an individual flat-owner would not be able to ask it to enforce another flat-owner's covenants which may not have been complied with. This is a fundamental principle of the lease relationship, which is a contract between at least two parties. Only parties to this 'contract' can be bound by it and, conversely, enforce it.

ALTERNATIVE STRUCTURES

With the increasing penalties falling on defaulting directors (see Chapter 11), methods of avoiding the problems of a flat management company as a limited company are being explored to see if the other structures will fulfil the desired capacity of pseudo-corporate status with less bureaucratic formalities.

MANAGEMENT BY THE FLAT-OWNERS THEMSELVES

Whilst there will always be situations where the flat-owners do not control their management company, many new developments are set up with the intention that at the completion of development the freehold ownership will, as a matter of course, be transferred to an already constituted management company.

MANAGEMENT AND ITS CONSEQUENCES

It is this scenario, ie the control of management by the flat-owners themselves, which will form the main content of the rest of this book. In theory, this scenario is the best situation for the flat-owners. As their own landlord, flat-owners can retain control and decide how to deal with problems as and when they arise. In practice, however, the situation may be quite different. Management will, essentially, be by committee. Not all flat-owners will have the same idea of how the company should be run. Some flat-owners will be non-resident, others will simply be apathetic and very often it may be difficult to persuade flat-owners to undertake an official role in the company to ensure its efficient running. The success of the management company will therefore depend on the firmness and control of the management committee and very often the thickness of the skins of its officers. The appointment of efficient professional advisers will also contribute to the successful running of the company.

Alternative methods of management

A further variation may be the granting of a concurrent lease to a management company which effectively exists alongside the freehold. Here, the flat-owners will contract with the freeholder and separately with a management company. At no time will the company hold any legal title in the building. The freeholder still retains certain rights over his legal interest and also his obligations in respect of his covenants under the lease, but only to the extent that the management company fails to comply with such covenants which have also been imposed upon it under the lease. The management company assumes the legal right to manage and collect the service charges. As to the flat-owners, they are relieved of the responsibility of management, but very often the problem arises that the freeholder retains the right to collect rents without any responsibility for management. The management company then has no income from ground rents and, consequently, may not be able to fulfil the obligations of management.

This form of management is like three layers of a cake, with the flat-owners at the top, the management company forming the centre of the cake, and the actual owner of the building comprising the flats on the bottom layer, ensuring that in most cases the owner has no involvement in the operation of the building but is merely providing a final safety net should the management company fail to fulfil its obligations.

Management companies and mortgage lenders

The effective management of blocks of flats has become an increasingly important consideration for lenders when lending on the security of a flat. Over the last few years, many lenders have specified that they will lend only where there is a management company structure in place. A badly run management company may well cause a valuer to give a reduced valuation on a flat. The latest guidance for solicitors when considering handling flat management is that, where a management company is required by a lender, the management company must own the land, the flat-owners must all be members of the flat management company and that company must be properly constituted and be filing annual accounts. The lease and the enforcement provisions must also be in an acceptable form.

What kind of management is best?

- The best kind of management is good management.
- The recognised and most common structure is the limited company.
- Who owns the company will often govern how well or badly management is controlled.
- Structures will vary according to the age of the block, where it is located, and the number of flats.

In London, for instance, there is a large preponderance of blocks in estate ownership, whereas in modern developing areas, blocks are set up with customised management companies handed over to the flat-owners when the development is complete.

When buying a flat, a buyer should always consider the management structure. Well-managed blocks are usually easier to sell and because they are well managed are likely to be more harmonious places in which to live.

CHECK-LIST

(1) What structure is in place to manage the building?
(2) Does the lease contain clear provisions to enforce obligations against the management company?
(3) If a management company is in place, does it own the building and can it therefore control the operation of the building?
(4) Has the company been run correctly and is it properly constituted?
(5) If no proper management company exists, should one be set up before the flat-owner proceeds to purchase?
(6) What requirements does the flat-owner's proposed building society require in respect of flat management?

Summary

A separate legal structure is usually necessary to manage the parts of a building owned in common by a collection of flat-owners, both for practical and legal reasons.

A variety of legal structures can be used, depending on the number of flats in a building and whether or not there is an external landlord. In some cases, if no structure is in place, the flat-owners may be able to acquire their building and set up their own management by law.

The main types of management structure:

criss-cross lease – a building with two flats where each owner owns the other's freehold;

owner-manager – where a landlord retains his interest in the block, often as a non-resident individual or company, and assumes directly the responsibilities of management imposed on him under the lease (now subject to compulsory deprivation of his interest by enfranchisement);

flat-owner management company – however acquired, the freehold interest of a block of flats vested in a limited company owned and operated by the flat-owners themselves;

concurrent lease – the flat-owners, freeholder and management company are all separate; the freeholder may collect rents but a separate management company controls the common parts of the property and carries out all the common obligations;

residents' associations – pressure groups representing residents' interests to an external landlord who also manages the property.

hapter **Two**

The Management Company

Incorporation

GENERAL

It is the landlord of any block who is responsible for management. Individuals or corporate bodies may own the freehold and in such cases management is the sole responsibility of the individual or corporate bodies.

Where there is collective ownership, a company is set up by the flat-owners which becomes the landlord and assumes the obligations of landlord under the lease. In such cases, the terms 'landlord' and 'management company' are interchangeable. An individual flat-owner has two legal interests in his property, as legal owner of his or her flat and as a part owner (by virtue of the shareholding in the management company) of the company which owns the freehold.

There will be cases where an individual or corporate body either chooses or is directly permitted by a lease to appoint an independent third party (paid for by the flat-owners) to manage the block. This external 'management' must be distinguished from the management company since it involved little or no involvement from the flat-owners themselves.

Large blocks may have a management company owned by the flat-owners which itself delegates day-to-day management to an external professional manager. Unlike in the previous paragraph this 'manager' is answerable to the management company.

This chapter focuses on the mechanics of the limited company itself. It is fundamental to the successful operation of a management company that a basic understanding of company structure and the statutory rules and regulations accompanying it is understood by those tasked with management.

DEFINITION OF LIMITED LIABILITY

A limited company is a distinct entity having a separate legal capacity from its constituent shareholders (or members). The company's members have control of the destiny of the company as they exercise their voting rights at general meetings, while the day-to-day control is vested in its directors (or officers).

It may be limited by shares or by guarantee.

Limited liability means that the liability of the members to contribute to the debts of the company is limited. Each member has either purchased a share in the company or guaranteed to contribute a fixed sum to the company. The amount which they have paid for their share or the amount which they have guaranteed is the limit of their liability to contribute to the debts of the company. Where the member has actually paid for shares, this is known as a company limited by shares. Where a guarantee only has been given, the company is referred to as one limited by guarantee. Many management companies are set up as companies limited by guarantee.

Liability for the debts of the company may be qualified in certain cases where directors are found to have exceeded their authority or continued to trade when insolvent. Since a flat management company does not trade, however, this latter consideration is not material.

LIMITED BY SHARES OR GUARANTEE

It is important to understand the purpose of limited liability and the difference between share companies and guarantee companies. It may affect the flat-owners' decision as to what type of company should be used for their particular purpose.

Share company

This form of company has an authorised share capital, the amount of which may vary widely, but in the case of a management company, may often be very small. Such a company usually has an authorised capital which directly mirrors the number of flats in the block. The company may then sell (or issue) up to that number in shares. This is known as the issued share capital. The company is not obliged to issue all of the shares, but must have at least two shareholders at all times to ensure it complies with the law.

Each share has a value attached to it and, in the case of a management company, each share will probably have a nominal value. This is the amount which each shareholder pays for the share or shares he or she buys. Upon payment, the applicant is allotted that share to which he or she is entitled and then becomes a shareholder or member of the company and is entitled to vote in that capacity.

In flat management companies limited by shares, each member will be entitled to a share on payment for it. It will usually be a condition of ownership of a flat that he or she must also be a member of the company.

When a flat-owner sells and moves, he or she will no longer be entitled to remain as a member of the company and will transfer his or her share to the new owner upon sale.

Guarantee company

In a guarantee company, no share certificates are issued. Each member is automatically entered on the register of members provided that he or she fulfils the necessary qualification for membership and applies for membership, and is removed when he or she no longer qualifies.

The principle of having to contribute to the liability of the company remains, but instead of the company having actual money in its hands (its share capital), each person who is a member of the company guarantees that, if called upon to do so, he or she will at that time contribute such amount as has been previously guaranteed by that member.

Whether a flat management company is limited by shares or by guarantee is often a matter of personal preference, but the guarantee company is more often used in smaller blocks and the share company in larger blocks. In practical terms, it may be administratively more simple to adopt the guarantee format, because it does not involve the physical transfer of shares each time a flat changes hands.

The procedure for transfer of shareholdings is dealt with in Chapter 9.

THE MANAGEMENT COMPANY CONTRASTED WITH A TRADING COMPANY

The function of a flat management company is to manage the affairs of a property and, generally, not to trade. It is essentially administrative and, as will be seen in Chapter 8 dealing with accounting procedures, the question of profit and loss should not, as a rule, arise.

Profits shown in the accounts of a flat management company not only have tax implications, but may also raise questions from individual flat-owners as to why profits have been made. After all, the monies to fund the running of the company are coming out of the flat-owners' own pockets and are provided only to cover the costs of the administration of the property.

In the same way, such a company should, in theory, not show losses. Officers of the company should budget sufficient funds from its members to finance its proposed activities without incurring losses.

In a trading company, shares become valuable commodities which can be bought and sold at values which reflect the profitability of the company. Flat management companies make no profits, and therefore the shares usually change hands only on the transfer of ownership of a flat and only at their face value. It is usually impossible to transfer those shares to anyone who is not a flat-owner.

Pre-formation matters

Before taking on the task of management, several matters must be considered.

WHEN DEVELOPER INCORPORATES THE COMPANY

In new developments, where the developer or his solicitor has thought ahead, the company necessary for flat management will be set up and incorporated before any flats in a building are sold. Many leases will contain a clause which states that, when the last flat is sold by the developer, its solicitor will deal (usually at no cost) with the transfer of ownership of the building comprising the flats and ensure that the developer relinquishes any interest in the company and hands over its future running to the flat-owners. The flat-owners in these situations will not need to consider any further the formalities necessary to incorporate a new company or the transfer of the building into that company.

WHEN FLAT-OWNERS MUST SET UP THE COMPANY

Where either the developer has made no provision for management or where a landlord has retained control of management, it will be for the flat-owners to set up a company when they acquire the freehold either voluntarily or by enfranchisement.

OBTAINING A CONSENSUS

As with all problems associated with the running of a flat management company, there is one factor which will be ever-present, namely the difficulty of obtaining a consensus of opinion amongst flat-owners as to what to do and when to do it.

In trying to reach agreement to form a company, those driving the proposal may find that some flat-owners may be non-resident and difficult to communicate with, while others may be simply apathetic. Success in organisation will normally depend on at least a few of the flat-owners having the will and perseverance to drive the matter forward. Even then, they may have difficulty in ensuring that a sufficient majority of the flat-owners are committed enough to enable the necessary actions to be carried out, particularly where enfranchisement is contemplated.

THE FORMATION COMMITTEE

Assuming that there are sufficient persons willing to proceed, they will usually form themselves into a committee with delegated authority to proceed with the arrangements for setting up the company and transferring ownership from the landlord to the company.

The formation committee's functions

USING PROFESSIONALS   **(for explanation of star-rating system, see Preface)

The formation committee is often unequipped to deal with the incorporation of their proposed company. Some committees may be lucky and have a resident solicitor or accountant who can do much of the work at no cost.

At an early stage, professional advice, both legal and accounting, should be sought.

In cases where the company is already incorporated and structured, the committee will ensure that, once the company is handed over to the flat-owners, the new officers are appointed (see Chapter 9). If this scenario is present, then the rest of this chapter is of passing interest only, since it will then be a case of following procedures for running the company at a later date.

If, on the other hand, the flat-owners have been offered the opportunity to purchase their own building or intend to enfranchise, the committee will be consulted by the solicitor appointed by it as to the structure of the management company, and it is then that consideration must be given to the appropriate type of company. The company formation will then proceed before the legal transfer of ownership of the building comprising the flats occurs either voluntarily or compulsorily.

It is important to remember that legal ownership of the building will be in the company being created and not in individual flat-owners.

INCORPORATION PRIOR TO TRANSFER **

It will be necessary to ensure that the company is incorporated prior to transfer taking place. Until incorporation, the proposed company has no legal capacity. It will be for the flat-owners' advisers to ensure that matters are dealt with in the correct order. This will involve the completion of forms (detailed later) and very often the use of company formation agents.

Incorporation (the date upon which the company is officially recognised as having legal capacity), is the date on which the Registrar of Companies issues a certificate of incorporation confirming that the company legally exists.

OTHER CONSIDERATIONS

The formation committee should ensure that all the supporting requirements of the company are considered and put in place:

(1) **banking facilities:** the committee should arrange the appropriate current account with a local bank, agree who should be signatories to the account, provide the signed mandates to the bank, set up a deposit account if monies are to be held on account for service charges;

(2) **appointment of auditors and accountants:** since accounts have to be produced and audited each year (see Chapter 9), involve accountants early so that systems can be put in place to make the job of the accountants as simple and cost-effective as possible;

(3) **location of registered office:** often the address of the building or one of the flats in the building;

(4) **printing of stationery:** unlikely to be necessary in all but the largest management companies, but some headed letter paper may be thought necessary if funds permit and in such cases the name of the company (including the word 'limited') should appear on the paper, along with the details of the location of the registered office and the company's registration number. It is not necessary to include the directors' names, as a flat management company may well have a rapid turnover of officers, which would involve constant and expensive reprinting.

COSTS

To buy a freehold, it will normally require payment to a landlord. Consideration will need to be given to the provision of finance for the acquisition, not only for the purchase price, but also for solicitor's fees and any stamp duty and other fees which may be payable.

The solicitor will be able to give guidance on the figures which should be budgeted for, for this element of the transaction, a matter which is of great importance, especially if not all owners have agreed to the acquisition. It is always more difficult after the event to obtain money from unwilling parties and it is therefore preferable to ensure that such matters are covered in advance. In the case of enfranchisement, this is particularly necessary (see Chapter 3).

Company basics

GENERAL

Any company has a set of formal procedural documents upon which rests its constitution. These are a set of rules and regulations which say what the company may or may not do. Collectively, these form a point of reference for the members of the company to ensure that the company operates only within its constitutionally permitted limits. Actions taken by the company outside these rules are open to challenge as being unauthorised and are known legally as 'ultra vires' actions.

Statute prescribes that a company cannot exist unless it has a Memorandum and Articles of Association to which the initial members of the new company have subscribed. It also requires certain forms to be filed at Companies House before the Registrar of Companies will issue the certificate of incorporation.

Until all these procedures have been complied with, a company cannot have any legal capacity, for example, to enter into any form of binding contract with others.

THE CERTIFICATE OF INCORPORATION

When issued, the certificate of incorporation gives the date of incorporation, and this is conclusive evidence that the statutory requirements of formation have been complied with.

It will need to be produced at certain times to establish this fact, for example to a bank which is to provide banking facilities to the new company.

If a company registered with a particular name wishes at any subsequent time to change its name, it may do so by special resolution, and in such cases a fresh certificate will be issued once the appropriate resolution has been filed which confirms that the change of name has been registered.

Outside parties have access to the register of companies and will, at any time, be able to verify the existence of a company which has been so registered.

THE MEMORANDUM AND ARTICLES OF ASSOCIATION

Although the company has its own legal status, it can act only through its members.

The Memorandum and Articles of the company regulate the activities of the company and its members.

The Memorandum deals specifically with the power of the company to deal with third parties. Its main purpose is to set out the objects of the company. These 'objects' may comprise a long set of clauses detailing, in particular, all those areas in which the company anticipates it will need to be authorised to operate and will often include some wider objects clauses to cover areas not covered elsewhere. Specific 'objects' will be included for management companies.

As well as setting out the purposes of the company, Memorandum clauses also state the amount of the company's authorised share capital, the fact that it has limited liability and the extent of each shareholder's liability.

The Articles are a set of rules to which the members of the company must adhere. They usually specify the method by which directors are appointed and removed, the appointment of a chairman, voting procedures, procedures at board meetings, regulations concerning the transfer of shares in the company, and so on. This represents the internal constitution of the company and often needs to be referred to when procedural questions arise.

Flat management companies will usually have specific provisions in their Articles regarding who can be members of the company and restricting membership only to persons who are owners of flats in a building.

Typical forms of Memorandum and Articles for use by flat management companies (both limited by shares and by guarantee) are included in Appendix 1.

THE REGISTRAR

The Registrar is the government officer authorised to certify that a company exists. Companies may be registered in England and Wales or in Scotland. Separate registries exist in Cardiff for companies registered in England and Wales, and in Edinburgh for those registered in Scotland. Any document which requires to be filed with the Registrar will need to be sent to the appropriate registry. The increasing use of the internet means that most searches of Companies House can now be carried out electronically.

STATUTORY REQUIREMENTS

The Companies Act 1985 specifies the procedural requirements of setting up a company and incorporation generally. It is possible for anyone to incorporate a company, but it is often simpler to use a company such as Jordans Limited who will set up ready-made companies 'off-the-shelf'.

Company formation specialists will have designed companies in which the objects' clauses and other provisions will be appropriate for a flat management company without need for major amendment.

Transferring ownership to the new company ***

OBTAINING GOOD TITLE

Whether compulsorily or voluntarily acquired, the new company's solicitor will ensure that good title to the building is obtained. Checks will be made on any matter which is likely to affect the future operation of the company and advice will also be given on the liabilities and responsibilities that the newly formed management company will be taking on.

Details of all leases into which the building has been subdivided will be obtained.

Unlike acting for a person acquiring a lease, the solicitor will look at the title from the other end, namely from the landlord's point of view, since those obligations as to maintenance, insurance and common parts, which previously the solicitor would have wished to ensure properly falling upon the original landlord, will, in future, be assumed by the new management company.

Provisions of the leases for collection of rent, payment of management charges, and provisions for collecting service charge payments now become of prime importance, for it will, in future, fall on the new management company to enforce collection of such payments. Any weak drafting or inadequate collection provisions can cause problems when confronted by unwilling or recalcitrant flat-owners.

INSURANCE

Prior to completing the transfer of ownership of the building, consideration will be given to insurance. The new management company may wish to take over existing insurance or may wish to obtain a number of quotations to obtain a cheaper premium.

RENTS

The solicitor will also enquire as to the current state of payments from each flat-owner. Are ground rents paid up to date? What provision will be made on completion for bringing any arrears up to date? Will it fall to the new company to take over responsibility for collecting any arrears?

Ensuring that these matters are dealt with at this initial stage is important, for, ideally, the new management company will wish to start operations without any historical problems, whether resulting from the outgoing owner's inefficiency or the flat-owners' reluctance to pay.

Indicating that certain flat-owners have, in the past, been slow to pay on demand is useful information for the future based on the principle that forewarned is forearmed.

Costs of formation

FINANCING THE COSTS OF FORMATION

Of course, like in all things, cost is an important consideration in the formation of the company and, as indicated before, it is a cost which will fall on the flat-owners themselves. It is a one-off cost and, for the purposes of financial reassurance, it may be advisable for the formation committee to obtain funds in advance from all flat-owners so that they are sure they will not foot the bill entirely from their own resources. This is not always easy, since the tangible benefits of owning their own building may not be immediately apparent to the average flat-owner. How much it costs depends on what needs to be done. There will be the costs of the acquisition of the company itself, whether off-the-shelf or otherwise. There will be solicitor's fees and various other fees such as stamp duty, search fees and land registry fees. In the case of flat management companies already set up by developers, the costs will have been absorbed in the development but, when starting afresh, all of these costs will fall on the flat-owners themselves.

The best advice is to ensure that the enquiry as to costs is made at an early stage. It will then be possible to build into the committee's budget a global figure upon which to base its calculations.

COMPLETION FORMALITIES

Once the company has been incorporated, the title has been checked and a date set for completion, it is time to spend the money which the committee has anticipated in its budget or to proceed with enfranchisement if necessary.

In the case of voluntary sale, the company's solicitor will make sure that everything is in order for the new company to take legal ownership of its own building. Insurance is transferred into the name of the new company, transfer documentation is completed and the solicitor will proceed to register the transfer of ownership.

Eventually, the deeds will be handed over to the company for safekeeping and future reference. At this point, all the waiting is over and the problems of day-to-day management begin. With luck, the structure will be sufficient for all future needs. Upon the structure can then be hung the formalities of management.

Taking stock

CHECKING LEASES   ✷✷✷

Brief mention was made earlier of the lease provisions. The committee's solicitor may have made mention of deficiencies in the leases.

Unfortunately, no two leases are the same. If the leases are inadequate, it is a good time, upon taking over, to consider whether it is necessary to vary their provisions. Except where a court order is obtained, variation cannot be effected unilaterally without the consent of the flat-owners as individuals.

IDENTIFYING AND RECTIFYING OMISSIONS   ✷✷✷

It is possible that the most important omission from the leases may be provisions for interim service charge payments or for payments by standing order or the provisions of a sinking fund.

As soon as possible after completion, a meeting should be called of all flat-owners. It is quite likely that the original committee may have previously handled all the negotiations with irregular reference to the other flat-owners. They will wish to know how things will change and it is an opportune moment to raise questions such as lease amendment or variation at this stage while matters are still fresh in the mind.

This is a fundamental principle which, if observed, will serve the board of directors well during the life of the company.

Consultation and keeping flat-owners informed will serve only to assist in heading-off complaints from aggrieved flat-owners.

Summary

- Decide the method of management which suits the property best.
- Use professionals when setting up a management company.
- Form a small formation committee to handle the initial phase of setting up the company.
- Ensure adequate formation finance.
- Consult and inform flat-owners of progress.
- Take the opportunity to discuss changes to leases and the methods by which change can be effected.

hapter **Three**

Becoming your own Landlord – Enfranchisement ***

Introduction

This chapter will address how the flat-owners in a block of flats can acquire collectively the ownership of their freehold title compulsorily.

The Landlord and Tenant Act 1987 went part of the way towards granting rights in certain circumstances to flat-owners collectively to acquire ownership of the freehold of their blocks but only on a 'first refusal' basis. This procedure will be covered later in the chapter.

Until the passing of the Leasehold Reform, Housing and Urban Development Act 1993, however, flat-owners were still frustrated by the inability to compel a landlord who was unacceptable to them to sell his interest to them – they remained effectively disenfranchised. The use of the word 'enfranchisement' (the right collectively to compel an unwilling landlord to sell) will as a result of the passing of the Act soon attain an important meaning in the consideration of a flat-owner's position by introducing a powerful new weapon in the flat-owner's hands. References in this book to 'the 1993 Act' will include statutory modifications subsequently enacted.

This chapter will go through the necessary steps to achieve enfranchisement. The fundamental problem will, however, still remain and that is the ever-present problem of how to harness the wishes and individual characteristics of a group of flat-owners, not least when presented with the prospect of up-front costs before any formal steps towards enfranchisement are achieved.

The matters contained in this chapter are complex and will always require professional assistance.

At the time of going to press, a new Bill proposing amendments to the legislation was in preparation.

Enfranchisement

PHASE ONE: INITIAL CONSIDERATIONS

A. Beginning the process

In this chapter, the focus will be more on the reasons for enfranchising rather than the mechanical process. This is largely because what the flat-owners are seeking to achieve by enfranchising is very important.

The reasons for enfranchising are many but here are a few of the commonest:

- bad or indifferent management by the landlord;
- excessively high management charges;
- long leases which are reducing in length need to be extended;
- changes required to the lease;
- inability to contact landlord when needed;
- landlord has disappeared;
- flat-owners simply prefer the idea of self-ownership.

Whatever the reason, it will probably be through the efforts of a representative core of flat-owners that the process will be instituted and driven.

Since the whole enfranchisement process will inevitably involve substantial cost, it is always worthwhile to attempt a direct approach to a landlord to ascertain whether the landlord may be open to a voluntary disposal. Sometimes, landlords are only too happy to pass on their interest, more especially where there is a disproportionate effort required by a landlord in relation to the benefit received. Where agreement can be reached, it is a relatively swift and straightforward matter to effect transfer. The unwilling landlord is often the landlord who earns substantial benefit from his position. Ground rents may be lucrative and there may be the possibility of earning commission on insurance or work for an associated company.

A word of warning in cases of negotiated transfers. If it appears that the negotiation is dragging on or that there is a likelihood of later prevarication by a landlord then it may be better to press on sooner rather than later with compulsory enfranchisement.

B. Project management

For successful enfranchisement, getting a good team together is very important. In small blocks, all members may take part in the team. With a larger block, a dedicated committee is preferable, reporting regularly to the other flat-owners and liaising with and instructing professional advisers.

Not all flat-owners will qualify legally to take part in the enfranchisement process but may still want to be involved in the new management company. Others may be reluctant to become involved. It may be wise to cover the situation of a flat-owner selling part way through the process. It is important in such situations to bind in together all those who are to take part. To lose a participant during the enfranchisement process can be dangerous since it may remove one of the qualifying conditions (see p 34). One of the first tasks of the steering committee should therefore be to prepare and submit a 'Participation Agreement' to all flat-owners. This contract will usually be drawn up by the solicitor acting for the flat-owners.

C. Assembling title information

The steering committee will need to check on legal ownerships, not only that of the landlord but also of each individual flat-owner. Most titles are now registered and it will be quite simple to verify most owners' titles. Correct identification of flat-owners is necessary to ensure the information on the initial notice is correct.

With the landlord, investigation at the Land Registry can be supplemented by various statutory notices that can be served on the freeholder and any other party requesting information on ownership and title. There are strict time-limits on such parties to reply.

D. Financial considerations

Whilst it is no longer necessary for a surveyor to give a valuation on the purchase price, the committee will need to know at this stage what the likely costs are going to be. To be aware at this stage of the value if the matter proceeds to a tribunal is vital. It also provides a basis for collection of money from flat-owners to finance the operation. The use of a surveyor specifically qualified in enfranchisement valuations is highly recommended.

E. Decision to proceed

When ready to proceed, the committee will then need to implement a series of preliminary steps:

- form a new limited company to act as nominee purchaser;
- send questionnaire to each flat-owner asking for specific periods of occupancy of the property and requesting funds;
- circulate participation agreements for signature;
- verify that qualifying conditions are achieved – see phase 2;
- set up bank account;
- collect funds;
- instruct solicitors to proceed.

PHASE TWO: CHECK QUALIFYING REQUIREMENTS

There are a series of qualification hurdles and in order for enfranchisement to proceed these criteria must be satisfied.

The right to 'collective' enfranchisement applies to a series of qualifying tenants (which makes it a collective right) in respect of a qualifying property. This is defined in the 1993 Act as 'relevant premises'.

Relevant premises

Premises to qualify must comprise together a self-contained building or part of a building. The freehold of that self-contained unit must itself be owned by the same person. There must be at least two flats which satisfy the qualifying tenant criteria (see below) within the self-contained building and at least two-thirds of the flats in the building must be qualifying flats.

To be self-contained as a building will normally be quite obvious but, in case of doubt, the 1993 Act states that division vertically will demonstrate this, enabling adjoining parts to be redeveloped independently. Additionally, where services are supplied to the unit independently of others or where they could be so provided without interruption of supply, this constitutes self-containment. By implication, buildings subdivided horizontally appear to fall outside the scope of the Act.

Qualifying tenants

A person is a qualifying tenant where he is the tenant of the flat and holds it on a long lease at a low rent. No flat shall have more than one qualifying tenant. Joint tenants shall be treated as a single qualifying tenant.

Long lease

A tenant must have a lease with at least 21 years to run before its contractual end date (plus a series of other less common special cases – consult a solicitor if in doubt).

Low rent

The rent in question is the original ground rent as stated in the lease. The question of what is 'low' depends on when the lease began. Having checked the lease for its start date and initial ground rent the following figures apply:

- For leases starting before 1 April 1963, the ground rent must not be more than two-thirds of the letting value of the flat on the day the lease began.
- For leases starting after 1 April 1963 but before 1 April 1990, the ground rent must not be more than two-thirds of the rateable value of the flat on the day the lease began.

- For leases starting after 1 April 1990, the ground rent for flats in Greater London shall not exceed £1000 and outside London £250.

There are certain technical provisions to deal with properties with nil rateable values and for those that do not meet the lower rent test (professional advice needed *).

Occupancy qualification

There is no residency requirement to become a qualifying tenant but there is one imposed at the stage of giving the initial notice (see p 33).

Exclusions from qualification

If the tenant owns more than two qualifying flats in a building, the tenant ceases to be a qualifying tenant. If the building has a resident landlord and there are no more than four qualifying flats in the building, no enfranchisement can take place. Where any part of the building is occupied or intended to be occupied for any other purpose than residential use, the building is excluded subject to the proviso that up to 10 per cent of the internal floor area of the building may be so alternatively used. (Internal floor area is calculated to exclude such areas as common parts.)

Tenants qualifying, building does not. What then?

Where by virtue of the exclusions above the tenants do not qualify then they may have a right to call for a 90-year extension to their lease (seek legal advice). This area is not dealt with in this book since it is outside the area of the actual running of a flat management company.

PHASE THREE: VALUING THE FREEHOLD

Assessing the price? A critical factor in deciding to proceed

The use of a surveyor is necessary to provide a valuation of the freehold. This will form the basis of the offer price contained in the enfranchisement notice. Clearly, if the valuation is substantial, this may cause the flat-owners to stop and consider whether the price is already too high to justify proceeding with enfranchisement.

The criteria for assessing the value of the freehold are set out below.

How a value of the freehold is calculated

Possibly the most daunting task of all is the assessment and calculation of the price to be paid for the freehold. A complete Schedule to the 1993 Act is set aside for the purpose of guiding the valuation process. It is essential that the help of professional surveyors is obtained in applying the formulae for arriving at a value.

There are, put simply, two elements to the price to be paid. The first is the market value of the freehold with willing buyer and seller discounting certain market elements. This is a not unfamiliar basis for market valuations and will certainly be familiar to a qualified surveyor. The second element is referred to as the 'marriage value' and a share of this figure is combined with the market value to make up the price payable.

Marriage value

The way in which the marriage value is calculated is complex and beyond the scope of this book. However, in simple terms, the marriage value is the increase in the overall value of the building resulting from the aggregation of the value of the freehold and all other constituent subordinate interests (largely the leasehold interests).

The share of this amount which is added to the freehold market value is either decided by a leasehold valuation tribunal or is 50 per cent, whichever is greater. In certain circumstances, there may be an additional figure included to compensate a landlord for loss of, for instance, a future development value.

Intermediate interests

Intermediate interests will also figure in a valuation calculation. Where there is some intermediate non-qualifying commercial interest, this may substantially increase the costs of acquisition making the cost of the enfranchisement more than it is really worth to the flat-owners.

PHASE FOUR: GIVING NOTICE

The notice claiming collective enfranchisement is given to the freehold owner by at least two-thirds of the qualifying tenants in the building. This is known as 'the initial notice'. At least half of the qualifying tenants who give notice must satisfy the residence condition (see p 33).

Initial notice

The initial notice must contain certain details as follows:

(a)   a plan showing the extent of the freehold building to be acquired by enfranchisement, identifying the way in which that building is subdivided into its compartmental leasehold parts and identifying any other parts of buildings in respect of which it will be required that the freehold owner grants rights necessary to the acquisition of the freehold of the enfranchiseable building;

(b) a statement of the grounds on which the tenants claim to be qualified to assert their collective rights to enfranchise under the 1993 Act;

(c) details of any intermediate leasehold interest to be acquired under the 1993 Act and details of any flats which may be secure or other types of protected tenancies as specified in the 1993 Act;

(d) a statement of the proposed purchase price incorporating within it any additional amounts such as for intermediate leasehold interests;

(e) a list comprising the names and addresses of all qualifying tenants and details of their respective legal interests to substantiate their status as qualifying tenants;

(f) details of the person or persons appointed as 'nominee purchaser' and their address;

(g) a date specified by which the freeholder must serve any counter-notice, such date falling at least two months ahead.

Once given, no further notice can be given whilst the first remains in force but, if withdrawn, a new notice may be given but not until at least 12 months have elapsed since the withdrawal of the previous notice. The notice ceases to be effective only if withdrawn, if a contract for sale under the 1993 Act is concluded (when it is superseded by other legal obligations in any case) or when other provisions of the 1993 Act are activated prompting cancellation of the notice.

Residence condition

A tenant achieves the residence condition if he or she has used the flat as his or her own principal residence for the last 12 months or for periods totalling three years in the last 10 years.

Who is bound by the initial notice?

The qualifying tenants are those listed in the initial notice and it is they who are the persons who participate in the enfranchisement process.

Intervening sale by a participating tenant

The 1993 Act has recognised the fact that flat-owners buy and sell and that a sale may intervene in the enfranchisement process. Where this occurs and the seller of the flat is one of those listed as participating tenants in the initial notice then there is a procedure specified for allowing the substitution or otherwise of the new owner for the old owner.

The new owner or his solicitors shall give notice of the change of ownership to the nominee purchaser within 14 days of the change and, if the seller had been a party to the initial notice, a statement of whether the new owner wishes to participate in the proposed acquisition.

A new owner may also buy from a seller who was a qualifying tenant but who had not joined in the initial notice. In such cases, a new owner may wish to be included in the acquisition and may elect to do so provided all the other participating tenants agree.

In either case, once notified of the new owner's wish to participate then the new owner shall from that time become a participating tenant until such time as he sells (or dies).

Death of a participating tenant

In the case of the death of a participating tenant, the trustees or executors of his estate have up to 56 days to decide whether to withdraw from participation and to notify the nominee purchaser of the death of the tenant. In the absence, therefore, of an election to withdraw there is a presumption of continuing participation.

Informing the freeholder of sale or death of participating tenant

Within 28 days of receipt of any notifications of sale or death of a participating tenant, the nominee purchaser is obliged to tell the freeholder of such changes and give notice also to any other intermediate landlords who may be involved.

The form of notice shall include all relevant details to update who becomes a substitute participator or who ceases to be a participator.

It is in theory possible that sufficient participators may elect to withdraw that the two-thirds rule fails. What happens if this occurs is likely to be the subject of future legal discussion.

Change of nominee purchaser

There are similar provisions to those above where it is proposed to change the nominee purchaser. In the event that the nominee purchaser is a limited company, these provisions are generally unlikely to be required.

PHASE FIVE: THE OWNER'S RESPONSE

Access for inspection

Any freeholder or other interested party (such as an intermediate landlord) has the right once an initial notice is received to have access to the property so that he can carry out a valuation. At least three days' notice must be given and it must take place at a reasonable time.

Moratorium on freehold disposal

Once the initial notice is received, the freeholder cannot dispose of his interest to anyone other than the flat-owners pending completion of the process, and if the property is already subject to a contract for sale, this is also frozen. This latter point will give outside purchasers of blocks of flats a great deal of concern, since they may already have had to satisfy the 'first refusal' hurdles imposed by the Landlord and Tenant Act 1987 and then find themselves frustrated in proceeding.

Right of owner to request information

The 1993 Act gives the owner the right to ask the nominee purchaser for evidence of a tenant's qualifications to participate in the enfranchisement process. A request must be made within 21 days of receipt of the initial notice and must be answered within a further 21 days from the date of the request. Failure to respond to the request by the nominee purchaser will result in the automatic withdrawal of the initial notice.

Service of counter-notice

The owner upon whom the initial notice has been served has the right to respond with a counter-notice to the nominee purchaser within the time-limits stated in the initial notice.

The counter-notice will acknowledge receipt of the initial notice and will contain either an admission that the tenants had the right to serve the notice and exercise their collective rights to enfranchise or, alternatively, it will state the reasons upon which the owner contests the validity of the tenants' claims.

Where the owner accepts the validity of the tenants' claim, the counter-notice will then state those items in the initial notice which are accepted by the owner and those which are not. For those items which are not accepted, the owner may make counter-proposals. The owner will also state the interest of other parties that it will be necessary to acquire and the rights that the owner wishes to retain over the property once it changes hands. All the information necessary to the conclusion of a correct legal transfer with associated rights to all interested parties should be ascertained as a result of the notice and counter-service.

PHASE SIX: NEGOTIATING AND APPLICATIONS TO COURT

Agreeing terms

In much the same way as the Landlord and Tenant Act 1987 supposed a period of negotiation stemming from the formal procedures, so it is hoped that under the new leasehold enfranchisement law a similar process will occur. It is probable, however, by the nature of the process that unwilling landlords will seek every assistance in the new law to avoid the transfer of ownership from themselves.

If the parties can agree, then the process will move to a contract and completion of transfer. If not, then the parties will have to resort to further formal procedures under the 1993 Act, either referring the matter to court or the Leasehold Valuation Tribunal.

Reference to court

The court can upon application make a declaration as to the validity of the tenants' claim to exercise collective enfranchisement, where an owner in the counter-notice has stated that the tenants do not satisfy the qualifying criteria. An application has to come to the court within two months of the date of giving the counter-notice.

If the court decides in favour of the tenants (through their nominee purchaser), the court order will declare the counter-notice invalid and require the service of a fresh counter-notice. If the court finds in favour of the owner then the initial notice fails and the enfranchisement process stops.

There are other procedures which may be invoked at various stages to resolve disputes, and it will be necessary to consult a solicitor for detailed advice on these procedures.

Leasehold Valuation Tribunal

Matters of dispute regarding acquisition terms may also be referred
to the Leasehold Valuation Tribunal for determination by either
party. Applications to the Tribunal must be made after two months
but no later than six months from the giving of the counter-notice.

The type of matters to be decided by the Tribunal are likely to
concern the type of interest to be acquired, the extent of the
property, the price payable and other provisions which may need
to be included in the legal conveyance.

No counter-notice

If no counter-notice is given within the specified time period, the
nominee purchaser will need to make an application to the court
who will decide the terms upon which a transfer will take place.
Such an application must be made within six months of the date
upon which a counter-notice should have been received.

Unknown owner

Where an owner is unknown, the court has power to make an
order vesting ownership in the qualifying tenants upon application
by them and upon the court being satisfied that such an
application is validly made and that all appropriate enquiries have
been made to establish the identity and whereabouts of the owner.

PHASE SEVEN: FINALISING MATTERS

In most cases, the enfranchisement process will end with the
conclusion of a binding contract between the parties followed by a
legal transfer of ownership. After that has occurred, the flat-owners
will find themselves, as other flat-owners, faced with the ongoing
responsibilities of running their flat management company.

At any time before a binding contract is concluded, the nominee purchaser may give notice to withdraw; if so, the costs incurred by the other parties will fall on the flat-owners.

As to the costs of enfranchisement generally, the nominee purchaser will be required to underwrite many of the owner's costs in deducing title, the preparation of copies of the title required by the nominee purchaser, valuations and the conveyance itself.

The final conveyance to the nominee purchaser shall transfer the freehold ownership to that nominee purchaser subject only to the incumbrances already agreed or ordered under the enfranchisement process. There are other provisions relating to such things as existing mortgages which will require the advice of the nominee purchaser's solicitor.

Extended leasehold interests

Where the criteria for collective enfranchisement are not achieved, the 1993 Act contains provisions allowing for the extension of existing leasehold interests and the rules for such enfranchisement fall outside the particular scope of this book (consult your solicitor).

The Landlord and Tenant Act 1987

RIGHT OF FIRST REFUSAL

The preceding part of this chapter dealt with compelling the owner to sell to the flat-owners and Chapter 2 outlined a situation in which the landlord had either made provision during the disposal of the individual flats for the ultimate transfer of the reversionary (or parent) interest to a management company run by the flat-owners themselves or had subsequently, by agreement, agreed to such a transfer. This may not always be the case.

In certain cases, a landlord seeks to pass ownership to someone else other than the flat-owners themselves. The flat-owners themselves, in the past, may not have been aware that this was happening and could often find themselves with a landlord whom they did not know and who proved even less satisfactory than the old landlord.

Provided that certain criteria are met, the Landlord and Tenant Act 1987 provides that a landlord cannot dispose of his interest without first giving the flat-owners themselves the right to acquire his interest.

In brief, where the 'landlord' of 'premises' which contain two or more flats held by 'qualifying tenants' wishes to make a 'relevant disposal' of those premises, he must, before offering them to anyone else, first offer to make the disposal to a nominee of the qualifying tenants. This is an obligation which cannot be avoided and any failure to make such an offer gives rise to legal rights of enforcement by the qualifying tenants. (Note: words in inverted commas have a special meaning in this context and are explained more fully below.)

Part I of the Act requires the parties to satisfy a series of criteria; these are essentially hurdles to be overcome which the flat-owner must understand and apply in order to invoke the provisions of the Act.

Various questions need to be asked and if the answer to any of the questions is 'no', then the Act will not apply:

(1) Do the premises fall within Part I of the Act?

'Premises' must consist of the whole or part of a building.
'Premises' must contain at least two flats held by 'qualifying tenants'.
'Premises' containing the flats must also have more than 50 per cent of the flats occupied by qualifying tenants.
'Flat' is described as a distinct set of premises which is divided horizontally from the rest of the building.

For example, the Act will not apply if:

- a building contains only one flat;
- the building contains two flats, one on the ground floor and one on the first floor, but one flat is empty or occupied by a non-qualifying tenant;
- there are four flats and only two are occupied by qualifying tenants, since there will not be more than 50 per cent occupation by qualifying tenants;
- the building comprises residential and non-residential parts (eg a business) and more than 50 per cent is used for non-residential purposes.

Thus, the first hurdle may be difficult to overcome. We will take a simple example to satisfy the first hurdle.

Example
The building is a four-storey Georgian house, subdivided into two maisonettes, one on the ground and first floors, the other on the second and third floors. The flats are divided horizontally, and both are occupied by tenants. The premises fall within the Act providing there is a 'landlord' and both tenants are 'qualifying'.

(2) Is the landlord within the Act?

'Landlord' is the immediate landlord of the tenants and also any superior landlord if the intermediate landlord is a tenant himself with a tenancy of less than seven years. Some landlords are exempt, including those of a public nature such as housing corporations and resident landlords.

In our example, if one of the flats is occupied by the landlord, the Act will not apply. However, if he lives elsewhere the Act will apply.

(3) Who are 'qualifying tenants'?

In the context of this book, almost all tenants will be qualifying. The flat-owners will hold their flats on long leases. The exception will be if the flat-owner holds more than one lease of flats in the building.

In our example, if both flats are let on long leases to different owners, they will be qualifying tenants and since they represent 100 per cent of the tenants, the Act will apply if there is a 'relevant disposal'.

(4) Is there a relevant disposal?

There are many exceptions to the basic principle of the disposal of the landlord's interest. In our example, the landlord is quite simply intending to dispose of his major freehold interest in the property by selling it. In general terms, if this is proposed as a commercial transaction, then the Act will apply.

The landlord proposing to make a 'relevant disposal' ignores the Act at his peril. Failure to serve the appropriate notices on the flat-owners will give the flat-owners enforcement rights as detailed in the Act. A third party being offered the landlord's interest would be well advised to satisfy himself that the landlord has first offered his interest to the flat-owners and that the offer has been turned down. There is also now a criminal offence if a landlord fails to give notice.

THE PROCEDURE OF FIRST REFUSAL

Once the landlord has decided to sell his interest, and all the conditions above are satisfied, the Act sets out the procedure to be adopted and, in effect, it sets in motion a negotiating procedure not unlike any other commercial negotiation which may succeed or fail at any stage. It is, perhaps, easiest to list each stage of the process.

(1) Landlord serves notice on qualifying tenants setting out:
   (a) the principal terms of the offer stating the details of the property to be disposed of, the nature of the landlord's legal interest in the property and the price required;
   (b) that the terms constitute an offer to the qualifying tenants which may be accepted by the required number of qualifying tenants (ie more than 50 per cent);

   (c) the period in which the offer must be accepted (at least two months from service of the notice);

   (d) that after the two-month acceptance period there will be a further two months during which time a person or persons may be nominated to take the landlord's interest.

(2) Within the first two months, a majority of the qualifying tenants can accept the offer, failing which the offer will lapse.

(3) If the offer is correctly accepted, then persons must be nominated during the following two-month period to take the landlord's interest.

(4) Instead of an acceptance, the qualifying tenants may serve a counter-offer and the landlord may then either reject or accept the counter-offer.

(5) The acceptance notice must be one notice served by the necessary majority of tenants and it must be in writing giving the names and addresses of all the persons serving the notice.

(6) There are detailed provisions for the procedures governing offers and counter-offers but if, ultimately, the parties fail to agree, then the landlord is free to dispose of his interest during the following 12 months provided that he does so strictly on the same terms as offered to the tenants.

(7) Once the parties have accepted the offer and the nomination stage has been complied with, the matter then proceeds as any negotiation up to exchange and completion. The Act itself sees no need to detail this stage since it assumes that by this time the parties have a mutually agreed objective.

Mention was made previously of the situation where the landlord ignores his obligations and sells to a third party without the tenant's knowledge. The flat-owners will soon discover this when notified that rent is to be paid to someone else. The Act provides the mechanism whereby the new landlord can be required to dispose of his interest back to the qualifying tenants on the same terms as he acquired the interest.

SUMMARY OF OTHER PROVISIONS OF THE LANDLORD AND TENANT ACT 1987

Since this book is primarily concerned with flat-owners running their own management company, it is not proposed to deal in detail with the other parts of the Act, although all of the provisions should be noted and are summarised briefly below.

- PART TWO: APPOINTMENT OF MANAGERS BY COURT
  Where a landlord is dilatory in his management functions, qualifying tenants can apply to the court for the appointment of a manager.
- PART THREE: COMPULSORY ACQUISITION OF LANDLORD'S INTEREST BY TENANTS
  Where the appointment of a manager is inadequate, the tenants may apply to the court for an order for compulsory acquisition of the landlord's interest by their nominee.
- PART FOUR: VARIATION OF LEASES
  Long leaseholders given the right in certain circumstances to apply to the court for variation of terms of their leases where the lease fails to make adequate provision for various matters such as repair, maintenance, insurance or service charges.
- PART FIVE: MANAGEMENT OF LEASEHOLD PROPERTY
  General provisions extending existing provisions in relation to service charges and the requirement of landlords consulting before incurring expenditure, and late demand for service charge payments.

Chapter **Four**
Taking over the Reins

Introduction

The previous chapters have concentrated on the actual task of transferring the ownership of the landlord's title into the hands of the flat-owners themselves. Much of this work will have been carried out by professionals on behalf of the acquiring flat-owners.

It often comes as a shock to the flat-owners when they finally achieve their desired objective, namely the control of their own destiny. Often the problem is made more acute by the assumption by the professional adviser that the flat-owners have a good idea of what is required of them to keep the new management company running smoothly. Unfortunately, this is a very unwise assumption. Left to their own devices, without guidance and help, the management company can soon fall prey to the many pitfalls of administration failure or even simple lack of attention.

By indicating that they wish to control their own destiny, the flat-owners must assume the responsibilities which go with this wish. It is not, in fact, a complicated operation, at least with regard to formal requirements, especially in view of the relaxation of such requirements introduced in the Companies Act 1989. What it does require is regular attention and organisation.

Of course, in addition, the company's main officers will need two other characteristics – tact and diplomacy. Success in the running of the company will often be judged not by the expertise of the company secretary in filing statutory forms, but in more mundane matters, such as making sure the dustbins are emptied regularly, or in keeping annual management charges to a minimum.

Appointment of officers

It is most likely that all flat-owners will be shareholders or members of the management company. This may give them visions of grandeur and they may take it upon themselves to interfere on a regular basis in the day-to-day running of the company.

However, as with all companies, the members, whilst collectively the owners of the company will delegate the day-to-day running of the company to its officers, ie the directors who are empowered under the terms of the company's Articles to make management decisions on behalf of the company.

This chapter will deal with how the new officers take over their roles in the company. The following chapters will specifically identify their duties and responsibilities.

The minimum requirement for a company in respect of its officers is two officers who together, can run the company's affairs (subject to final approval of the members).

The two required officers are:

(1) *Director* – only one director need be in office at any one time. However, this may lead to an autocratic and impractical way of running a company and it is more common to appoint at least two directors. The director, or board of directors, can be appointed and removed by the members and can be reappointed on a rotating basis each year if so required. Provisions governing the appointment of directors and their removal are usually contained in the Articles;

(2) *Company secretary* – the administrative officer of the company. The company secretary has the most work to do, giving notice to the members of meetings, preparing notices, drafting resolutions, preparing minutes and filing all statutory forms.

When the company is handed over to the flat-owners, it is likely that the officers appointed initially will have been appointed to enable the handover to take place. These officers may have been the most active flat-owners and are possibly the most suitable for the job.

First meeting

Most flat management companies are best run by a small group of flat-owners acting as a committee, and they themselves may delegate certain administrative functions to sub-committees to look after specific jobs. An example will help at this stage.

EXAMPLE

A block of flats is divided into 12 flats. There is a separate garage block and a large forecourt area, a separate dustbin area and large landscaped gardens. The block also has common staircases and lifts, and is comprehensively insured through the management company. All of these matters have, until handover, been looked after by the original landlord (not very well) and the takeover of ownership of the building has been completed. (It is assumed for the purpose of this example that all the flat leases have comprehensive provisions permitting the management company to collect rent, service charges, insurance premiums, etc and also that ownership of all common parts will remain in the company's ownership and responsibility.)

Negotiations have been carried out by two flat-owners (Jones and Smith), who have been appointed director and company secretary. They have also taken transfer of one share in the company (Flatco Limited) each.

Thus: Flatco Limited

SHAREHOLDERS:	*2 – JONES and SMITH*
DIRECTOR:	*JONES*
COMPANY SECRETARY:	*SMITH*

Upon takeover of ownership, Jones and Smith first issue shares to all other flat-owners. If shares are £1 each, they will collect £1 from each of the other ten flat-owners at an initial meeting of the flat-owners and issue the ten further shares to those flat-owners. Thus, all flat-owners will become members of Flatco Limited.

Thus: Flatco Limited

SHAREHOLDERS	*12*
DIRECTOR:	*JONES*
COMPANY SECRETARY:	*SMITH*

At the first meeting, Smith explains that during the next year he will be away abroad working and cannot, therefore, carry out the company secretarial functions satisfactorily and offers his resignation to the members. He has already noted that there is an accountant called Brown who lives in a neighbouring flat who will be able to prepare the annual accounts cheaply and is willing to carry out the day-to-day bookkeeping. Brown has been primed in advance to offer his services as company secretary and his offer is put to the meeting. The members approve the new appointment.

Jones then invites members to volunteer their services as directors. After an explanation of how little work it will involve, three further directors are appointed who will form the committee of management for the forthcoming year. Jones explains to Hughes, Williams and Clarke that they will not be paid for their services and the meeting elects Jones as chairman. Jones explains that Brown's first task as company secretary will be to file at Companies House the notice of resignation and appointment of new officers. (Form 288, see Chapter 9.)

Thus: Flatco Limited
SHAREHOLDERS   12
Board of management
DIRECTOR: JONES (CHAIRMAN), HUGHES,
                            WILLIAMS and CLARKE
COMPANY SECRETARY: BROWN

The directors inform the meeting that before any further business is carried out they will have to meet and investigate the requirements of the flat-owners as to day-to-day management, and will call another meeting as soon as they can to report back.

That first meeting is crucial for it sets the tone for the future running of the property by the management company. It is an ideal opportunity for those who had initial responsibility for setting up the takeover of ownership to convince the other flat-owners that it is in everyone's interest to play an active role in the running of the company. If it is impossible to convey such a message, then it is likely that those few people will continue to do all the work, possibly with little thanks and much criticism. Whilst it may not be advisable to conduct any substantial business at an initial meeting, it is essential that the new officers are aware of what to do, and how to answer any questions which may arise. These questions are likely to be fairly predictable, most likely to do with leaking roofs, what sort of expenses are going to be incurred during the year and so on. (A check-list is contained in Chapter 10.)

It is important not to go into too much detail at this first meeting to avoid committing the management company to courses of action which may later prove unnecessary.

It is advisable at the first meeting to identify other areas which need to be resolved, such as the location of the company's registered office, any changes which may be necessary to the company's Articles (probably unlikely) and changes of directors, but keep these matters to a minimum at this stage to ensure that the legal requirements are all in order, leaving the more practical problems until later.

With the first meeting over, the structure is now in place. The new board of management may choose to set up small working committees to oversee various aspects of management, especially in the case of larger blocks of flats. These may be set up at the meeting or put together over a period of time by invitation or coercion.

If the flats are few in number, it may not be necessary for these committees to do very much other than the occasional administrative function but, whatever the number, it is important to try to maintain a regular system of meetings and regular communication. It is up to each individual company to ascertain its own requirements.

One other point of note at this stage is to emphasise the keeping of records. Not only does the law require the keeping of statutory books, but it is most useful to keep detailed minutes of meetings to document and record decisions. Reference to such minutes often saves a lot of time and dispute later on.

Assessing the functions of the company

Above all, it is important not to rush into making any commitments. This has been said already and is worth repeating. Many management companies find themselves rapidly bogged down in a mass of detail quite unnecessarily. In fact, it is counter-productive and leads to the creation of jobs out of all proportion to the needs of the company. It is the period after setting up the structure of the board which is vital. It is a period of assessment and familiarisation.

Summary

- The board and its respective members will now have satisfied themselves of their own responsibilities and with this information can begin to allocate responsibilities for each task and plan the future day-to-day running of the company.
- It is only the beginning, where the understanding of obligations is superseded by the politics of man-management and of keeping the flat-owners happy.
- At the heart of running a flat management company is the combination of efficient systems to manage the company's affairs, combined with an expertise in the art of disciplining a group of widely differing people who make up the membership of the flat management company.

Chapter Five
The Lease

Introduction

The relationship between individual flat-owners, and between them and the owner of the building of which their flats form a part, is integral to regulating matters between them. Without a formal document, no party would be able to identify individual obligations or enforce them against anyone else.

Across the world, different structures have been invented to cope with the concept of shared ownership. In Britain, historically, the lease has developed over many centuries as a method by which property owners can be given a legal title to land and buildings in respect of which it is impossible to give a simple freehold title. It is often difficult for the layman to understand why this should be so, and is made all the more difficult because of the length and complexity of many flat leases. In addition, because no two leases are the same, it is always necessary to study a particular lease in detail to identify any special provisions which it may contain.

The lease will always contain certain fundamental elements which are identified in this chapter, as well as specific provisions relevant to the particular building in question.

Leases are always produced in duplicate and the copy known as the 'counterpart', which has been signed by the flat-owner, is held by the landlord, and all counterparts form part of the management company's title to the property. In all but a few cases, each lease for a particular building will be in identical form. If the leases prove not to be identical in all material contents then it will probably be the first job of the management company to consult its solicitors to deal with deeds of variation to correct any anomalies. This is often a complicated and time-consuming (not to mention expensive) exercise and, with luck, anomalies should have been brought to the company's attention during the acquisition phase.

The lease

A brief explanation of a lease is to describe it as a contract between two parties – the landlord and the tenant – in which each party's rights and duties are set out. Duties are usually referred to in a lease as 'covenants', and each party will assume various obligations towards each other. The substance of the lease is in these covenants and their presence or absence will determine the effectiveness of being able to enforce the other's obligations.

Each form of lease generally has a similar structure, with variations largely resulting from the individual solicitor's drafting procedure. Some leases may be very sloppily drafted and others so long and complicated that they may result in pages and pages of unnecessary wordage. Whatever their form, they will need to be read and understood by both parties.

The flat-owner should have had the lease's provisions explained when buying the property and should be aware of the obligations he or she has taken on. The flat-owner will have had imposed upon him or her an obligation to pay ground rent, a service charge contribution and a series of regulations which are mostly based on practical common sense as to how to behave in the flat, and keeping the flat in good repair and condition.

What provisions must the management company look at?   *

(1) THE FLAT-OWNER'S OBLIGATIONS ('TENANT'S COVENANTS')

The regulations contained in the lease are contained in a series of numbered paragraphs, regulating everything from where to hang the washing to what kind of carpet must cover the floor. In general, these covenants will be self-explanatory and comprehensive. As a rule, many of these covenants will never need to be policed by the management company, although from time to time a dispute may arise between flat-owners where the company may be asked to adjudicate and enforce, for example, where there is a provision preventing the keeping of domestic pets, and a flat-owner is keeping a cat without authorisation.

The main covenants which the management company will be interested in are those relating to collection of income to pay for complying with its own obligations. These are:

(a) *Ground rent* – each lease will include a clause obliging the flat-owner to pay an annual payment to the landlord. Because most flat-leases are 'long leaseholds' running for a period of years, anything from 50 to 999 years, the ground rent is normally a nominal sum, perhaps £25 or £50 per year, and it may only be a peppercorn rent. (This is in fact a device meaning that no monetary rent is payable.) In the case of an outside landlord, this sum represents a small income which is for his benefit only and not for the use of the management of the property. Historically, these ground rents were quite saleable items and specialist investors often acquired large collections of ground rents which produced substantial incomes. In the situation where the flat-owners through their own management company have acquired their property, this rent is in fact a payment to themselves collectively and in these cases may not be regarded as income but may simply be used as a vehicle for subsidising the costs of maintenance and insurance. Thus, in the example previously mentioned, assuming a ground rent per flat of £25, there will be a fund of £300 available to the management company to go towards its costs.

(b) *Service charge* – for the management company this is a vital provision. Without it, the management company will have no redress against the individual flat-owners for recovery of the costs it incurs in fulfilling its obligations on behalf of its members. There are some leases where little or no thought has been given to the drafting of this clause and flat management companies should beware of such situations, even to the point of avoiding taking on management obligations. Flat-owners' solicitors and building societies will usually insist that such clauses are comprehensive to avoid the problems of inadequate management brought about by the realisation that the costs of such management may be difficult to recover. The clause itself may take two forms, either separating the obligation to pay a proportion of the insurance premium for building insurance and for general maintenance and upkeep, or rolling both into one all-embracing provision for reimbursement. It may also provide for a reserve or 'sinking fund'.

The board of management will note that its obligations will involve an element of expenditure, and with a comprehensive service charge collection provision, its concern about covering such costs will be relieved. Collection of service charges will always be one of the major problems encountered by a flat management company and will inevitably require the advice and assistance of a solicitor in the case of truly recalcitrant payers, but the production of clear estimates and final service charge accounts will go a long way to minimising the difficulties to be encountered.

(2) THE MANAGEMENT COMPANY'S OBLIGATIONS ('THE LESSOR'S COVENANTS')

Generally, after many pages of lessee's covenants, the landlord or lessor's covenants are short and to the point and cover those areas of responsibility which fall on the owner of the building. The main provisions are:

(a) *Quiet possession* – this clause is inserted in every lease, generally unqualified in any way. In essence, it means that so long as a flat-owner complies with his obligations, the lessor has no right to interfere with the flat-owner's occupation and ownership of his property.

(b) *To insure* – it has been recognised for a long time that it is impractical in a building subdivided into smaller units, which rely on each other for support and protection, to impose the obligation to insure on each individual flat-owner, since failure by even one flat-owner to insure his part may render it impossible to cover insurable risks effectively. Therefore, it is an obligation imposed on the lessor to cover the structure of the building (including common parts) with a block policy of insurance. The lessor is then able to recover a proportionate part of the premium payable against each flat-owner under the flat-owner's obligations under the lease. Frequently, the first duty of the newly formed management company is to ensure the transfer of insurance arrangements from the original landlord to itself and to satisfy itself that the amount of cover is sufficient to cover the cost of rebuilding in the event of total destruction of the premises.

(c) *To maintain* – whereas the duty to insure is a once-a-year obligation on renewal of the existing insurance arrangements, the duty to maintain is a continuing obligation and the one which will continually preoccupy the board of management. The lease will not only impose the obligation to maintain but also define the extent and nature of the maintenance services to be provided. Returning to the example of Flatco, these obligations will extend to the main fabric of the building comprising the flats, its drainage, its roof, its foundations, its common parts including staircases, lifts and entrance halls, the landscaped gardens and the forecourt areas. The costs of such maintenance will then be recoverable under the service charge obligations of the individual flat-owners.

(d) *To produce accounts* – flat-owners will expect their payments of service charges to be used for the purposes for which they were paid. In order to regulate this, annual accounts are normally required to be produced under the terms of the lease. This is a separate obligation from the statutory obligation to file annual audited accounts when the management company is a limited company. Certified and audited accounts will generally be required each year to be presented to the flat-owners, and their respective proportions identified. There may also be provisions whereby the management company can set up a sinking fund into which flat-owners pay monthly or other periodic payments to cover the estimated charges for the forthcoming year. There are usually provisions whereby they either receive a refund at the end of the year if they have overpaid or make a further payment to make up any shortfall.

There may be other specific provisions in certain leases depending on the nature of the property.

Summary

-   The vehicle which regulates the relationship between flat-owners is known as a 'lease'.
-   The lease is a contract in two parts, one held by the landlord and one by the flat-owner.
-   Without a lease, obligations between the flat-owners and the owners of the building become impossible to enforce.
-   Leases will vary according to the building but will normally contain specific provisions regarding rent, insurance, maintenance, and other rules of behaviour during an owner's occupation.
-   A solicitor should ensure that the obligations contained in the lease are clear and effective. If not, it may be necessary to amend the provisions of the lease to ensure efficient management of the flats in a building and to permit proper enforcement of those obligations should it prove necessary.

Chapter **Six**

Officers and their Duties

Introduction

This chapter will define the position of flat-owners as members of the flat management company, and contrast this position with that of the company's officers. This is an important distinction to understand in the make-up of a limited company, whether a flat management company or any other limited company. The officers of a company are its directors and company secretary.

Members and their duties

The company is defined as a legal entity in its own right – it has what is known as a legal 'personality' and it comprises its members, or shareholders, who exercise ultimate control over the company.

Members have rights which are attached to each share in the company. These are generally specified in the company's Articles of Association, which are in effect the company's rules and regulations. Among the common provisions will be the right to vote at members' meetings, also called general meetings and, in the case of flat management companies, the qualification that only flat-owners themselves may be members of the company. There are likely to be provisions that when a flat-owner sells a flat his or her share must be transferred to the new owner upon completion of the sale.

In general, each member will have one vote at a general meeting, although some weighted voting provisions may be included where some flats are larger than others and then each member may have proportionate voting entitlements.

Directors

The limited company is an artificial legal entity in the sense that it has no power to fulfil its functions itself. Some person or persons must therefore represent the company and carry out its functions.

It is this function which directors perform, either individually or collectively with others.

Private companies require only one director to be appointed. The term 'private' refers to any company which restricts ownership of the company to a limited class of persons and all flat management companies are likely to fall into this category. Flat-owners will normally be advised that more than one director should be appointed so that a 'committee decision' on matters relating to the running of the company may be reached. It also serves the practical function of maintaining continuity of administration when a flat-owner sells and retires as a director.

Directors are usually appointed at the annual general meeting or at other times when the need arises. In the case of a flat management company, this may arise each time a flat-owner sells.

Directors should check the provisions of the company's Articles for any specific provisions for rotation of directors on an annual basis.

Directors' functions

The Companies Act 1989 does not define what directors are or what their function is. The company's Articles normally provide that 'subject to the provisions of the Act, the Memorandum and Articles of Association and to any direction given by special resolution, the business ... shall be managed by the directors who may exercise all the powers of the company'.

It will clearly fall to the directors of the flat management company to assume responsibility on behalf of all flat-owners to ensure proper management of the property and to carry out the wishes of the majority of members expressed at members' meetings.

Directors are obliged to exercise their duties in the best interests of the company upon whose behalf they act and to comply with all statutory requirements.

It is not often that the directors will have cause to be over-concerned by the majority of statutory requirements by virtue of the administrative and non-trading nature of a flat management company, but they are best advised to familiarise themselves with any provisions which may affect such relevant duties.

A director, once appointed, may be removed by general meeting, by a majority vote of the members. This is a necessary procedure should an officer of the company prove to be incapable of carrying out his or her functions properly.

Usually, more than one director is appointed in a flat management company. Collectively, these directors comprise and are referred to as 'The Board of Directors'.

The board of directors

The board will operate on a committee structure with provisions for majority decisions at board meetings (Table A – Appendix 1, Forms 13 and 14).

Directors will normally choose their own way of regulating proceedings and request board meetings through the company secretary. As they begin to work together they will gradually adopt the procedures which suit them best. A chairman of the meeting is usually appointed who will normally hold a casting vote at meetings in the event of deadlock. Provisions for appointing alternative directors may also be permitted (if, eg, a director is abroad at the time of a meeting).

A 'quorum' is the number of directors below which a meeting becomes invalid and such number may be provided for in the Articles or fixed by the directors. The Articles usually provide that minutes of each board meeting are kept to note the names of all officers present, details of all proceedings and, when necessary, the appointment of new officers.

If a chairman is appointed, the directors may remove him at their majority wish or appoint another in his or her place. Such appointment is noted in the minutes of the meeting. The function of the chairman is to preside over the meeting and when necessary to exercise a casting vote.

It is unlikely, in the case of a management company, for each director to have a specific title (eg managing director) but it is often the case that each director is allocated specific areas of responsibility in connection with the administration of the property.

No remuneration is usually allowed for management company directors but provisions may be made for expenses to be paid in certain circumstances if the members consider it appropriate. This, and certain other functions, may be authorised only by the members in general meeting.

Allocating directors' duties

Depending on the number of directors on the board, several of the functions may need to be performed by one director. However, in larger blocks of flats, it may be possible to delegate specific areas to sub-committees to ease the workload of a particular director.

Common administrative requirements of a flat management company include:

(1) insurance;
(2) maintenance and repairs;
(3) banking;
(4) rent and service charge collection;
(5) preparation of annual budget estimates;
(6) maintenance of books of account;
(7) annual audit and annual accounts;
(8) security of property;
(9) keeping flat-owners informed.

(1) INSURANCE

This is an important requirement in respect of any property. In a block of flats, the individual leases will usually impose insurance responsibility on the landlord. This responsibility extends to the main structure of the building and to public liability. The service charge provisions will usually permit recovery from each flat-owner of a proportionate part of the insurance premium payable.

The director with responsibility for insurance will need to ensure that each year the amount of insurance cover is sufficient to cover total rebuilding costs. He or she will also usually be required to demonstrate that the premium payable is competitive and that the insurance company is reputable. Frequently, such policies have a sum assured which increases on an index-linked basis each year.

Insurance responsibilities

The director dealing with insurance will need to remember the following points:

(a) renewal of insurance annually;
(b) dealing with claims under insurance;
(c) negotiating with insurers;
(d) liaising with those responsible for maintenance;
(e) obtaining quotes for work to be done;
(f) when necessary, review current insurance to ensure sufficient value of building cover, and obtain comparable quotations from other insurance companies.

A further requirement may be made by individual flat-owners' building societies requiring their interest to be noted on any insurance policy. The director should ensure compliance with any such request if one is made and notify the insurer accordingly.

Failure to maintain adequate insurance could result in a severe financial burden on flat-owners in the event of damage occurring to the property.

(2) MAINTENANCE AND REPAIRS

Once the building is owned by the flat management company, the main structure of the property will usually become its responsibility. This includes the foundations, external walls, joists, roof and other supporting structures. The common parts, such as staircases, lifts, halls and main accessways will, also, usually be the company's responsibility. In addition, if there are communal gardens or yards and driveways, these will need to be maintained and managed. The director with responsibility for these matters will sometimes find this task onerous since the cost of maintenance and repairs features high in the list of costs which the flat-owners will ultimately have to share.

The director dealing with maintenance and repairs will need to remember the following points:

(a) assess the nature and extent of the company's responsibility for maintenance and repairs from the lease;
(b) obtain quotations before work is done;
(c) appoint contractors when necessary to carry out such work;
(d) seek the approval of all or a majority of the flat-owners before work is put in hand (except in an emergency);
(e) anticipate, and advise of, any major future expenditure for inclusion in the annual budget.

He will also need to liaise with the director involved with insurance and with the person whose job it is to prepare annual expenditure estimates.

Failure to inform flat-owners of substantial costs in connection with repairs before they are carried out and obtaining their approval can often lead to difficulties for the management company in recovering the cost of such repairs from flat-owners, notwithstanding that their leases allow the landlord to recover such cost.

(3) BANKING

The receipt of money from flat-owners, both as rent and service charges, requires the setting up of a bank account with cheque cashing and payment facilities. Usually, a simple current account will suffice, but if provision is made for a 'sinking fund' (money held on account in respect of anticipated expenditure), a deposit account earning interest may also be advisable.

The director responsible for banking will usually hold the mandate for cheque signing. It is essential, however, in such cases to ensure that the mandate requires at least two authorised signatories to prevent possible misuse of company funds. It is usual to provide that several authorised signatories are notified to the bank to avoid the problem of some signatories not being available when a cheque is required to be drawn.

The director in charge of banking may well be the same as the person dealing with maintaining books of account.

(4) RENT AND SERVICE CHARGE COLLECTION

All the financial functions of the company may be exercised by one director. There are always some recalcitrant payers amongst flat-owners. The director may find collection easiest by persuading flat-owners to make regular payments into the bank by way of standing order on a monthly basis. This also saves the problem of flat-owners having to find a single large lump sum when a major item of expenditure occurs.

Service charge statements will be related to the annual budgets prepared in respect of anticipated expenditure and will be corroborated each year on the presentation of the annual accounts. (A model service charge account is set out in Appendix 1.)

(5) PREPARATION OF ANNUAL BUDGET ESTIMATES

The director who takes on this task will have to assess, each year, the likely costs to be incurred in management over the next 12 months. He or she will liaise with the directors dealing with insurance, maintenance and repairs to estimate likely costs. Such budgets are usually presented just before the annual general meeting so that they can be considered by flat-owners and then discussed at the meeting before being sanctioned by the meeting.

Where very heavy additional costs are anticipated, it is advisable for the director to notify such anticipated expenditure as far in advance as possible to soften the blow to individual flat-owners. Major costs may be spread over several years and, sometimes, flat-owners may agree to such expenditure being financed by a bank loan, repayable over a period of time out of the flat-owners' service charge payments.

(6) MAINTENANCE OF ACCOUNTING RECORDS

This function will probably be performed by the same director who deals with other financial matters. Bookkeeping involves maintaining records of payments and receipts which will be used by the auditors and accountants when the year-end audit is carried out and accounts prepared. More will be said on this topic in Chapter 9.

(7) ANNUAL AUDIT AND ANNUAL ACCOUNTS

Accountants will be required to perform these tasks and the procedures and requirements in this regard are dealt with in the chapter on accounting requirements.

(8) SECURITY OF PROPERTY

Frequently, this function will be performed by the director who deals with maintenance and repairs. Very few security requirements will be necessary in small management companies, but larger blocks of flats may require extensive security arrangements.

(9) KEEPING FLAT-OWNERS INFORMED

It is recommended that one director is delegated with this task, specifically, on the principle that by keeping flat-owners well informed of what is going on with the property, the board will be making its job much easier. Most of the problems of dealing with fellow flat-owners result from the failure to communicate effectively and clearly what exactly is being done on behalf of them by their administrators.

The company secretary

As well as having at least one director, the company must have a company secretary. The company secretary is appointed and removed by the board of directors in accordance with the procedures set out in the Articles.

In management companies, the company secretary will normally be appointed from the ranks of the flat-owners themselves, but this is not obligatory. Sometimes, an outsider such as a solicitor, accountant or a professional agency such as Jordans Limited may be appointed if no flat-owner can perform the function satisfactorily.

If there is only one director, then that director cannot also be company secretary. There must be, at all times, at least two officers of the company.

In a flat management company, the company secretary's function is often critical. He or she is the company's chief administrative officer. Many flat management companies have been struck off because the company secretary has failed to appreciate the importance of his or her role in keeping the company's statutory books up to date and filing the appropriate forms at Companies House.

The company secretary's duties

There are a series of duties which a company secretary must assume as his responsibility. These are:

(1) convening board and company meetings as directed by the board (see Chapter 7);
(2) preparing minutes of meetings of the board and of general meetings (see Chapter 7);
(3) keeping the company's statutory books up to date (see below);

(4) filing returns at Companies House (see below and Chapter 10);

(5) cancelling and issuing share/membership certificates (see below and Chapter 10).

In addition, the company secretary has ostensible authority to bind the company in respect of contracts entered into on a day-to-day basis, say, for example, if a contract is placed to repair part of the property or in arranging insurance on behalf of the company.

Many of the obligations listed are important because, if they are not complied with, a 'default' occurs which could give rise to a fine.

Of the functions listed above, the first two will be described in more detail in the following chapter which describes the proceedings of meetings.

The formal functions of the company secretary will now be dealt with in more detail. The list is not exclusive and omits many functions which will rarely, if ever, arise in the case of a flat management company.

Keeping the statutory registers

The statutory registers (or books) refer collectively to the records which the law requires a company to keep, giving details of the company's structure and membership, and which are kept available for inspection by other shareholders and members of the public if and when required.

The contents of the various registers within the statutory books will (or should be) directly mirrored by the register maintained at Companies House. These will be updated by information filed by the company secretary on the occurrence of certain events such as the issuing of new shares, appointment and resignation of officers of the company and the filing of annual returns.

The register, which is usually in a folder (often in loose-leaf form), consists of a series of registers or folios in each of which material events are recorded. Often, in addition, the minutes of meetings are recorded in these registers or in a separate minute book.

THE REGISTER OF DIRECTORS AND COMPANY SECRETARY

Each director and company secretary appointed is listed in the register and certain other details are recorded. When a director or company secretary is appointed or removed, this is entered and the appropriate form recording the change is sent to Companies House.

THE REGISTER OF CHARGES

If the company mortgages its property to a third party (eg a bank), the company secretary must send notification to Companies House for registration and details will be entered in the appropriate folio or register. It is not often that flat management companies give such forms of security.

THE REGISTER OF MEMBERS

All shareholders (flat-owners) are entered on this register and changes noted when new flat-owners become members. The register shows each transfer of share ownership. There is usually a section containing blank share certificates or membership certificates which will be issued by the company secretary to each new member of the company.

OTHER REGISTERS

Other registers are also required, most of which will not generally concern the company secretary of a management company. However, it should be noted that directors of a limited company are required to disclose any share interests they may have in another limited company. A separate register is kept to record such interests.

FORM FILING

The list of forms which need to be filed at Companies House is lengthy and most will not concern the company secretary of a management company. (Those which specifically concern the company secretary are referred to at the appropriate points in the book and are reproduced in Appendix 1.)

PUBLIC INSPECTION OF REGISTERS

It is a legal requirement that the registers of all limited companies must be available for outside inspection. In order for this to be possible, members of the public need to know where such registers may be inspected. To this end, it is provided that the registers must be kept at the registered office of the company.

SHARE CERTIFICATES

The company secretary will maintain the membership register of the company and record the change in membership as and when a flat-owner leaves and another moves in. The procedures to be adopted are set out in Chapter 10.

Summary

- A company can function only through its officers. The officers of the company are its directors and the company secretary. Directors are collectively referred to as the board.
- The directors' duties will be administrative and cover all the responsibilities imposed on a landlord in respect of the building containing the flats. These may be determined from the provisions contained in the lease.

- The company secretary is an important officer whose duty is primarily to ensure the maintenance of the company's formal records and statutory registers, and to file the appropriate forms at Companies House when required by law to do so.

Chapter **Seven**
Directors' Meetings

Calling a board meeting

There is little or no formal requirement for the calling (sometimes called convening) of a meeting of the directors of a flat management company. If necessary, guidance will usually be found in the Articles. Invariably, such meetings will take an informal structure, at one of the directors' flats.

Board meetings will usually be called to discuss routine matters arising from day-to-day management of the flats or when there is a particular problem which needs to be decided which the director responsible does not want to decide on his own.

The board may make such rules as it wishes for the convening of such a meeting, and any director may at any time specifically request a meeting either himself or through the company secretary.

It is usual to require that a reasonable amount of notice (usually seven days) is given of such meetings, if only to ensure that the necessary quorum is present. The Articles usually provide for the appointment of alternative directors in place of any directors who are, for example, away at the time of the meeting, so as to ensure a quorum.

As a matter of practice, if the board is comprised of a number of directors, it is sensible to set out an agenda which is circulated beforehand, so that time is not wasted at the meeting deciding what to talk about.

Directors of flat management companies should aim to have at least one meeting every six months to review the way in which general management is proceeding, but each management company should adopt such meetings as the size of the management company and the administration of the company requires. Smaller flat management companies may not feel the need for anything more than the annual general meeting held each year.

Proceedings at directors' meetings

In the previous chapter the duties of each director were determined and specified. Much of the function of each director will be carried on without need for further sanction at board level.

The directors' meeting may simply consist of a series of reports from the directors on matters arising from the performance of such day-to-day functions. Specific problems may have arisen which a director feels should be aired at such meetings and directors can then present a united front when questions are asked of them by the members.

The company secretary will attend such meetings and keep minutes of what occurred and what decisions were reached, and the minutes of the last meeting will usually be produced for approval and signature.

Some decisions may have to be put to a vote of the directors present if agreement cannot be reached. In such cases, a simple majority of those present will be sufficient, with the chairman holding a casting vote in the event of deadlock.

A useful procedure to be adopted at meetings is to incorporate within the minutes an 'action list' which specifies to which director a task has been allocated to be carried out before the next meeting. This serves to concentrate the director's mind to the carrying out of a specific task, and ensures that matters do not get overlooked.

If a quorum of directors is not achieved, then the meeting should not take place and an alternate date should be set to reconvene the meeting.

The chairman

As explained previously, a chairman is usually appointed by the board to oversee proceedings at directors' meetings. Certain proposals may be put by a director which cannot be agreed without a majority authorisation before being actioned. The chairman may then hold the casting vote.

Since the chairman can exercise ultimate power in these situations, it is necessary to ensure that his method of election is clearly provided for in the Articles of the company, although in most circumstances it is unlikely that any major contentious problems will arise in the day-to-day running of the company.

The appointment of the chairman and duration of his or her term of office will be set out in the Articles and his appointment and removal minuted by the company secretary.

Contents of minutes

The minutes are the record of the business of a directors' meeting. It is usual that such minutes will record the names of those attending the meeting and detail apologies from those not present. The substance of the minutes will be to record decisions reached by the directors at the meeting and, as such, will not record the contents of the discussion which may have taken place.

The minutes will be drafted, usually by the company secretary, following the meeting, and then presented at the subsequent meeting for approval. If an 'action list' is incorporated, then the company secretary will draw the attention of the directors to those items requiring action to ascertain if such actions have by then been carried out.

The minutes are best kept in a folder or a bound volume and will usually be kept by the company secretary alongside the statutory books. Unlike other statutory records, the minutes of directors' meetings are not open to external inspection. Therefore, it is not essential that they be held with the other records, but usually, for convenience, they are kept together.

Delegation of directors' functions

The board may choose to create sub-committees from amongst the flat-owners to carry out certain administrative functions or to assist them in carrying out their duties. This may help to relieve the directors from assuming the whole burden of responsibility for managing the company's affairs.

Such committees will require supervision from the directors since, ultimately, it will be to the directors that the flat-owners as members of the company will look to explain decisions made by such persons acting under their authorisation.

Summary

- A board meeting is the forum for directors to discuss and decide matters of policy in respect of the flats and their management.
- Meetings may be called by any officer when necessary and matters raised at such meetings incorporated in an agenda.
- An 'action list' carried forward from meeting to meeting is a useful way of checking that matters specified to be done by officers of the company are, in fact, carried out.
- The chairman appointed will have the casting vote in the event that there is a split vote of the directors at a board meeting.
- Decisions are often made by agreement, but if there is no agreement the majority vote prevails.
- Some directors' functions may be delegated to sub-committees.
- Minutes should be kept of all board meetings.

hapter **Eight**
Shareholders' Meetings

Preliminary considerations

Meetings of the shareholders or members are known as general meetings. General meetings of a company are those occasions where the formal business of the company is conducted. This is contrasted with directors' meetings which primarily deal with the mundane day-to-day matters of administration.

Since the only function of a flat management company is administration, it may seem that the general meeting of the members is a mere formality designed to ensure that the formal requirements of running a limited company are complied with. Where flat management companies comprise few members, then it is quite likely that all flat-owners are also officers of the company and the general meeting is a mere formality. To say, however, that general meetings of all flat management companies are a formality is to underestimate their importance as a vehicle for flat-owners who are not officers of the company to have their say on how the appointed officers are managing their collective affairs. It is therefore important that in these cases the method of calling general meetings and the proceedings to be conducted at them are fully understood.

What is a general meeting?

A general meeting of a company is a meeting at which all members of the company are entitled to attend and at which they are empowered by virtue of the rights attaching to their membership to vote on certain matters.

There are two types of general meeting: the annual general meeting (AGM); and the extraordinary general meeting (EGM).

The annual general meeting   *

Once, each year, the directors of a company will submit themselves to the scrutiny of its members. It is obligatory for a company to hold an AGM of its members once in every calendar year.

The first AGM of a newly incorporated company need not be held until 18 months after incorporation, but no later than 18 months. Each subsequent AGM occurs annually with no more than 15 months between each such meeting. The flat management company is obliged, like any other limited company, to comply with this obligation to hold an AGM.

At the AGM, the directors may be questioned by the members and called to account for their handling of the affairs of the company throughout the year. Experience shows that, particularly in the case of larger flat management companies, the scrutiny and examination carried out of the directors at the AGM can be extremely comprehensive. The management company director approaching such a meeting unprepared does so at his or her peril.

CALLING AN ANNUAL GENERAL MEETING

As with an EGM (see p 81), it falls to the company secretary upon the request of the directors to send out the notice convening the AGM.

As a matter of policy, it is recommended that in the case of flat management companies the AGM is held as close to the same date each year as practicable. The date of such meeting should, ideally, be shortly after the end of the financial year so that accounts may be approved and budgets for the forthcoming year sanctioned.

The notice compiled by the company secretary states the following details:

(1) a statement that the meeting is an annual general meeting;
(2) details of the date, place and time of the meeting;
(3) an agenda of the business proposed to be dealt with, including the wording of any resolutions which are being proposed;
(4) details of rights of members to appoint proxies to vote.

(A 'proxy' is where a person entitled to vote at a general meeting, ie a member of the company, being unable to attend personally, confers formally upon another named individual, or the chairman, the right to vote on his behalf. It may also contain an instruction as to how the proxy should vote on a particular resolution.)

This notice is served on all members, directors and the auditors of the company. Notice must be given at least 21 clear days prior to the date of the AGM. If accounts are to be presented to the meeting for approval, copies of these accounts should be circulated with the notice convening the meeting.

The company secretary will want to ensure that all formalities are complied with. Any failure in formal requirements renders the notice invalid. In many flat management companies, there are 'barrack-room lawyers' just waiting to pounce on any failure to comply with formal requirements.

As with an EGM, if every member agrees, then the meeting may be held at short notice without the required 21 days' notice period having to elapse.

CONDUCTING BUSINESS AT THE ANNUAL GENERAL MEETING

The usual business of the AGM is as follows.

(1) The election of officers

The directors may be required by the Articles to retire by rotation each year. Those retiring may put themselves up for re-election and others may seek election.

(2) Presentation of accounts

The annual accounts and the auditor's report will be presented to the meeting and approved. It may be that members will require detailed information from the directors to explain discrepancies between budgeted expenditure and expenditure actually incurred during the year. The directors will probably wish to take the opportunity of presenting a budget of anticipated expenditure for the coming year.

(3) Appointment of auditors

The meeting will usually confirm the reappointment of the auditors for the coming year unless new auditors are to be appointed, in which case this will also be laid before the meeting for approval.

(4) Directors' reports

The directors may feel it is appropriate to lay before the meeting written reports on their area of responsibility during the year or to explain certain matters which may be of relevance to the members. To cite actual examples, in the case of a block of flats by the sea with its own marina, it was necessary to seek approval for substantial expenditure to repair sea defences during the coming year. In another case, antiquated sewerage facilities had to be improved to comply with new control of pollution regulations. Sanction for the expenditure had to be obtained from the members.

OTHER BUSINESS AT THE ANNUAL GENERAL MEETING

As well as the formal business of an AGM, which is explained below, it is not unusual for flat-owners to air every grievance which has built up over the year, and much time can be spent on discussing seemingly unimportant matters which to one member may appear life-threatening. It pays for directors to anticipate such grievances in order to avoid lengthy and unnecessary proceedings, not to mention the ill-will which can be generated by such discussions.

Directors should also note that some discussion can be avoided where no proper resolution has been proposed and included on the agenda of the meeting.

ATTENDANCE AT THE ANNUAL GENERAL MEETING

As said before, a formal AGM is necessary only where the flat management company comprises a large number of flat-owners. In such cases, all members are entitled to attend and they should be provided with facilities to permit their attendance at a suitable venue. The Articles will provide details of the quorum required to pass any resolutions proposed.

The company secretary will record details of all those attending the meeting. There must be a quorum. The chairman of the board of directors will, if in attendance, chair the AGM.

VOTING

Voting may be by show of hands, unless before, or on the declaration of the outcome of a show of hands, a poll is requested.

The chairman, or two shareholders, or one shareholder holding at least one-tenth of the company's issued share capital, may demand a poll.

A shareholder on a poll vote usually has one vote per share held. Only shareholders in person may vote on a show of hands. In the case of a poll, proxies may vote.

MINUTES

As with a directors' meeting, minutes must be kept of the AGM and any other general meeting. These will record those attending, the proceedings, and any resolutions passed. They will be signed at the next meeting by the chairman as a true record, and kept with all other company records.

The company secretary will have to file any special resolutions or forms, such as for the appointment of new officers at Companies House after the meeting as required by the Companies Act 1985. (See Appendix 2 for addresses.)

COMPLETING THE ANNUAL RETURN **

It has been seen that the records kept at Companies House are designed to mirror those kept at the registered office of the company. However, whilst the company secretary is obliged to file certain changes which occur during the year with Companies House, such as changes of directors, there is no obligation to record changes in the membership of the company each time one occurs. This, of course, could be frequent in the case of a flat management company where flats change hands on a regular basis. In addition, the accounts of the company can be filed only once a year after they have been prepared.

The accounts and the annual return must be filed at Companies House annually to maintain the records correctly. Until recently, the biggest cause of companies being struck off the register was because of failure to file either or both the annual return and the annual audited accounts. The obligation to file accounts remains unchanged but, under the new regime, computerised reminders will be sent to companies when such accounts are due to remind the company secretary of his obligations in this respect.

The annual return is sent to each company from Companies House, and on it is reproduced the current information held on the register in respect of the company. It is then a simple matter for the company secretary to compare the details shown against his own up-to-date statutory books, amend the return where necessary, and return the amended form to Companies House, duly signed by one director and the company secretary, together with the appropriate fee. The annual return should be made up to a date not later than the anniversary of the formation of the company or the anniversary of the last annual return if different. (See Chapter 10 for further details on filing the annual return and Appendix 1 for form of annual return.)

The extraordinary general meeting ***

Any meeting of members other than the AGM is known as an EGM. In many flat management companies, an EGM is hardly ever necessary. It is usually required only in circumstances where a decision of the members is required which cannot wait for the AGM.

The board of directors may summon an EGM at any time by instructing the company secretary to call the meeting. Members representing at least one-tenth of the voting rights of the company may also request such a meeting – this is known as requisitioning a meeting and is effected by the deposition of a formal requisition at the company's registered office. Such a requisition, if valid, will oblige the directors to call an EGM.

Why, in the case of a flat management company, an EGM should ever be necessary, depends on the circumstances surrounding the director's intention in calling such a meeting.

The notice calling an EGM will specify the business which needs to be discussed. This may include such matters as altering the articles of the company, the winding-up of the company or the removal of a director.

The formalities of calling an EGM are as follows.

(1) The company secretary prepares a notice specifying the date, time and place of the meeting, detailing the business which is proposed to be transacted, including resolutions to be proposed, and reminding shareholders of their right to appoint proxies.
(2) The notice is then sent to each member.
(3) Depending on the type of resolution which is being proposed, a notice period must be given.

(4) In certain circumstances, the notice period may be dispensed with, where a majority of the members who are entitled to vote, and being at least 90 per cent of the total membership, agree.

The business is then transacted at the EGM by the shareholders voting on such resolutions as are proposed.

Written resolutions

Small private companies, and especially flat management companies, now have the facility to dispense with the actual holding of a meeting. The Companies Act 1989 introduced procedures whereby private companies may pass resolutions without the need for an EGM so long as every shareholder or member entitled to vote agrees. In such cases, every shareholder signs the written resolution consenting to its terms. Subject to certain exceptions, unlikely to be of concern in the case of flat management companies, such a signed resolution is as effective as if passed at an EGM. A copy of the resolution is retained and, if required, it must be filed at Companies House within such period of time as may be specified in respect of particular resolutions.

Elective resolutions **

The Government has recognised the fact that many private companies do not need to involve themselves in some of the more formal procedures of running a company, and certain matters may now be dealt with by an elective resolution of the members. By the passing of such elective resolutions, the members may relax certain statutory requirements.

Smaller flat management companies may decide that the actual holding of a formal AGM is quite unnecessary. Provided that all shareholders agree, they may pass an elective resolution permitting the company to dispense with the holding of an AGM. The passing of such an elective resolution will be revoked by a later ordinary resolution, but will remain in force until such a resolution is passed.

If a shareholder wishes that an AGM should be held in a particular year after such an elective resolution has been passed, then he or she may require the holding of such meeting provided that due notice of such request has been made prior to the end of September in that year.

Elective resolutions may also be used:

(1) to permit the company to send the annual accounts to members for approval rather than lay them before a general meeting for approval;

(2) to dispense with the annual reappointment of the company's auditors;

(3) to reduce the percentage of shareholders' consent to hold an EGM at short notice to a minimum of 90 per cent.

In the case of a flat management company, the members may feel that it is important to retain the AGM since it is the one occasion during the year when all members have the opportunity to comment on the running of the company.

PASSING AN ELECTIVE RESOLUTION

To pass an elective resolution, a general meeting of the company is held at which all members must be present and they must all agree to such a resolution being passed.

The use of the written resolution procedure may also be adopted to pass the elective resolution, but professional advice is recommended before adopting this procedure.

Conclusions

This chapter has dealt with the most important event in the year of the company. The general meeting is the means by which the members of the company can, in effect, scrutinise the running of the company. It demonstrates that with an efficient administration and structure the flat management company can survive such scrutiny without undue criticism. Failure by the directors to run the company in an efficient manner will only make their life difficult, especially where the management company is made up of numerous flat-owners. The art of flat management is striking the balance between efficiency, tact and diplomacy, and it is an art which may never be completely successful. By following a few simple disciplines, however, problems can at least be minimised.

Summary

- A general meeting is a meeting of the members of the company, at which formal business of the company is carried out.
- All members are entitled to attend and vote at such meetings. They may also appoint a proxy to attend on their behalf.
- Two main types of general meeting are available: the annual general meeting; and the extraordinary general meeting.
- Resolutions are voted on at general meetings.
- Written resolutions are a method by which members can approve proposals without the necessity of a formal meeting.
- Elective resolutions permit the company to dispense with certain statutory requirements usually required of the company.
- Procedures at an AGM are detailed in the check-lists contained in Chapter 10.

Chapter Nine
Financial Management and Accounts

Introduction

In some respects, a flat management company is like any other business and as such it is important to run that business on a sound financial basis. The only real difference is that it is unlikely that the company will be trading and, therefore, will not be concerned with making profits. However, the mere fact that the company is not trading does not free it from the requirements of good financial management or from the statutory requirements of preparing accounts.

It is important to distinguish between the maintenance of adequate accounting records of a day-to-day nature, and 'accounts'. Accounting records are the books and records which are kept by the company as evidence of the company's financial transactions. They are for internal consumption and will provide the basis of decisions made by the company in respect of expenditure and budgeting. Accounts are drawn up by professional accountants at the end of each financial year, and in the case of a limited company they are audited. They are based on the accounting records and represent a point-in-time summary of the financial state of the company. These are required by statute and will be produced at regular, usually annual, intervals, for filing as a public record.

The two aspects of financial record-keeping are mutually interdependent, for without regularly maintained accounting records, it will be very difficult for the company's accountants to produce the end-of-year accounts.

Being non-trading, a flat management company is permitted certain relaxations in the presentation of its accounts. This will simplify the work which needs to be done by the company's accountants, resulting in their preparation being significantly cheaper than those prepared in respect of a trading company.

Without accounting records, the company will cease to be an efficient unit. Keeping records of expenditure for maintenance of property shared by several or many flat-owners will be vital in ensuring that questions raised about the extent and level of expenditure are capable of justification and explanation.

Keeping the day-to-day accounting records of a flat management company should not prove too arduous for the large majority of such companies. If there is an accountant resident in the building, he or she may be volunteered for the task of maintaining those records. Larger flat management companies may feel it prudent to employ the services of a regular bookkeeper; an expense which the owners may agree to share amongst themselves, and also the use of a managing agent (often a firm of chartered surveyors) who will be charged with the function of preparation of annual maintenance estimates and the collection of payments.

The preparation of the annual statutory accounts cannot be carried out by a layman and will require the appointment of a professional firm of accountants who are required to 'audit' the accounts prior to their finalisation and filing. Auditors are appointed by the members of the company in general meeting and their position reaffirmed at the AGM.

This chapter will provide an overview of the day-to-day matters of financial management and an outline guide to the statutory accounting requirements.

Income

The flat management company will need income to pay for the expenditure it incurs in carrying out its obligations to the collective group of flat-owners. Income will not come from trading receipts, since the company has nothing to sell. It will come only from the flat-owners themselves who together make up the membership of the company.

In the example used in this book, it is assumed that the company has no external ownership and, as such, the company is wholly under the control of the flat-owners. Provided that a decision is taken by a majority of the members of the company, that decision is usually unchallengeable. Questions of who pays for what are also, usually, clearly defined and set out in the terms of the individual leases.

There are two types of income: the ground rent; and the service charge.

GROUND RENT

Every lease has a provision for some sort of annual payment known as 'ground rent' or simply 'rent'. This rent is usually small and forms the appendix in the body of the property. It is relatively insignificant and is largely a historical hangover. However, no matter what the size of this payment, it is still a regular and enforceable payment. The accumulated value of a large number of small rents can result in a substantial income.

Ground rent is payable to the owner of the building. In the case of a company which is wholly owned by the flat-owners, the rent is, effectively, being made in part to themselves as members of that company. In cases where the owner is another person, this rent is income for whatever purpose the owner sees fit. In the flat management company, the members could collectively agree that they will not enforce the collection of this rent. However, they may, instead, agree that this sum, collected regularly, will provide the basic 'working capital' of the company – a form of sinking fund to provide against the company's expenditure. This would reduce the amount which the company has to collect, additionally, by way of service charge.

SERVICE CHARGE

The service charge is the sum of money which the company will need to collect from all flat-owners on a regular basis to pay for the expenditure incurred by the management company in carrying out its obligations as to insurance, maintenance and repairs. If ground rent is absorbed as part of this cost, then it will represent the only source of income of the company, and in a well-run management company will be equal to the expenditure incurred. It may produce a small surplus in some years, often intentionally in advance, where the company has foreseen a major item of expenditure at some time in the future and is collecting monies on account to relieve the pressure of having to pay a large sum all in one payment.

Expenditure

Expenditure is defined simply as the money laid out by the company in servicing the property. In very small flat management schemes, it may be as little as the insurance premium in respect of the building, and a small sum to cover minor items of maintenance or repairs. At the other end of the scale, it may be substantial and cover major items of structural repair, the hiring of contractors to carry out works at the property, the commissioning of professionals to carry out architectural, planning, financial, legal or other services, the employment of managing agents and so on.

Whatever the extent of the expenditure, the company will have to justify the expense to its members. It will be required to lay regularly before its members details of such payments. In larger companies, where many of the members are not actively involved in the day-to-day running of the company, it is likely to be the subject of detailed scrutiny and often criticism, especially when such expenditure directly involves the flat-owner in the payment of large sums of money. It is not unknown for flat-owners to perceive certain items of expenditure as unfair, such as where it appears that their payments are being utilised for the benefit of some, but not all, flat-owners.

Where expenditure proposed exceeds certain limits, the tenants must be served with a notice giving them a right to object (seek professional advice *).

The collection of service charges by management companies is subject to statutory provisions enabling flat-owners to challenge these through various courts and tribunals and, in such cases, professional advice should be sought. This area is outside the general scope of this book.

Balancing the budget

At the end of each year, the income and expenditure of the flat management company should be in balance. There may be small 1989 sufficient funds to cover the costs of carrying out its obligations on behalf of its members.

For all management companies, large or small, it is prudent to apply sound principles of financial management by estimates of anticipated future expenditure for budgeting purposes and the maintenance of proper accounting records. In this way, the company is run in a happy and efficient way and without being open to excessive criticism for making rash expenditure decisions.

Maintaining accounting records **

Unlike a trading company, the actual task of maintaining 'the books' in a flat management company is very simple. In smaller companies there may be very few entries during a year, and even in larger companies there will not be the complications of wages, PAYE, VAT or other similar matters. The books, therefore, will simply hold a record of income received and payments made. A simple cash-book system will suffice for recording such transactions.

The 'cash book' records all transactions through the company's bank. It is split into a series of columns in two sections identified as income and expenditure, known as 'credits' and 'debits' respectively.

The company's accountants may advise that, in larger companies, separate ledgers are set up to record details of specific types of transactions which will enable rapid identification of total expenditure in particular areas of the company's operation. This may also facilitate the preparation of interim management accounts without the need for analysis of the cash-book entries.

The production of interim management accounts is necessary only in larger management companies where there is substantial expenditure each year, and where the officers of the company wish to extract at certain points during the financial year a summary of income and expenditure, to date, to compare this against the figures budgeted at the beginning of the year.

Management companies (especially those which are too large to deal with records manually and which are too small to employ outside managing agents) may wish to use one of the many proprietary accounting packages available for use on computer which are relatively cheap to install and simple to use.

Accounting records need to be retained for inspection, for a period of years, for various purposes, and so should be in a form which lends itself to retention. Whilst it may not concern most management companies, the company should be aware that HM Customs & Excise (VAT) require records to be retained for six years, and the Inland Revenue for seven years.

Types of accounts

A clear distinction must be drawn between those accounts drawn up for the internal consumption of the management company, and the statutory accounts prepared annually for public record.

MANAGEMENT ACCOUNTS

Management accounts are internal accounts produced from time to time by the directors for their own purposes, such as to compare budgeted expenditure against actual expenditure. Very small management companies will probably find these unnecessary. A few simple payments each year will be recouped from the flat-owners when they fall due. Medium-size companies may find it appropriate to draw up six-monthly management accounts, if only to enable the directors to ascertain whether they are likely to need to ask for more money to cover unbudgeted or unusual expenditure. The largest flat management companies may wish to produce monthly management accounts, if only for the directors' information. The production of such management accounts may also be used to produce estimated accounts for the coming year, so that the level of service charge contributions for the following year can be assessed in advance. It is always easier to collect money in advance than having to collect monies after the event.

STATUTORY ACCOUNTS ✱✱✱

As opposed to management accounts, statutory accounts are the accounts specified by law as having to be prepared and audited each year for all limited companies and made available for public inspection. The company has no choice in their production, and failure to prepare them will result in unwelcome consequences, such as the striking-off of the company (see Chapter 11), and penalties in the form of fines for directors of the company.

The accounts, once prepared, must be filed at Companies House. They will then be open to the inspection of the public as a matter of record.

The accounts must be audited by the company's auditor. This must be a firm of accountants who are qualified as either certified or chartered accountants. There is, therefore, no way to avoid the necessity of paying for the cost of the production of such accounts. It should be noted that the auditors of the company are empowered to require from the company's directors any information which they need to carry out their audit.

The format of statutory accounts is regulated by legislation. Trading companies are required to produce a profit and loss account for the accounting period, a balance sheet, a statement showing the source and application of funds, and notes to the accounts explaining various matters. As has been noted previously, the flat management company is a non-trading entity and will, therefore, not have a profit and loss account. In such cases, there is an exemption permitting the filing of a simplified balance sheet and certain accompanying notes. Almost all flat management companies will be able to avail themselves of this relaxation but, if in doubt, guidance should be sought from the company's accountants.

The audit ✱✱✱

The audit is a process of review of the accounts which have been prepared by the accountant. It is usual, but not imperative, that the accountants who prepare the annual accounts also perform the audit function. The management company may have a qualified accountant as a flat-owner who has him- or herself prepared the actual accounts, which are then submitted to the auditor for review. The auditor checks figures against documented paperwork and accounting records to satisfy himself that the accounts present a true and accurate record of the company's financial transactions.

Once completed, the auditor will attach an audit report to the accounts stating his belief as to the veracity of the accounts. If there are any qualifications to the accounts, these will be stated in the report. Most reports from accounts which are regularly maintained will result in an unqualified report.

Tax returns

Most management companies' liability for tax will be negligible, and in most cases will be irrelevant. It may, however, be necessary to file annual tax returns and the company's accountant will advise on this when the accounts are prepared.

Distribution of statutory accounts

Once prepared and audited, the accounts are laid before a general meeting of the company and approved by the members. The members may have dispensed with the necessity of an AGM (see Chapter 8) by the passing of an 'elective resolution' or of approving the accounts in general meeting and, in such cases, the accounts are simply circulated to each member.

Having been approved, the accounts are then signed by the directors of the company and submitted to Companies House for filing on the public record. They must be filed, in the case of UK companies, no later than 10 months after the end of the relevant accounting period (see Chapter 10).

A copy of the accounts is provided to each member and a further copy is usually retained with the company's statutory books for reference purposes.

The need for proper accounting procedures

For the directors of the flat management company, complete and accurate accounting procedures are essential.

Management accounts will facilitate the easier justification of expenditure to individual flat-owners and assist in the preparation of annual estimates for the forthcoming year. They will also reduce the cost of using professional accountants.

The preparation of statutory accounts and the auditing of them will be simpler and therefore cheaper for the management company. It will also avoid the likelihood of an audit producing a qualified report from the auditor.

Directors should be aware of the financial consequences of failure to comply with the filing of the statutory accounts each year and the possibility upon failure of disastrous consequences leading to the ultimate striking-off of the company itself (see Chapter 11 for details of penalties on directors).

Summary

- Efficient maintenance of a flat management company's financial situation is important both for the members themselves and in order to comply with legal requirements.
- Proper accounting records should be kept by the company no matter how few the transactions in any year. This helps to keep the cost of the annual preparation of the company's accounts to a minimum and makes it easier for the auditors to give an unqualified 'audit report'.
- Internal management accounts may be produced if the company's size justifies their preparation to assist the officers of the company in keeping a check on the actual cost of maintenance, etc as against the budgeted estimates at the start of a year. They may also assist the officers in answering specific queries on them raised by members.

- Statutory accounts must be prepared annually, be certified by the company's auditors and filed at Companies House. Failure to do so will result in penalties on the officers and possible striking-off of the company.

hapter Ten
Company Secretary's Check-lists

Introduction

There are many aspects of running any company where it will be essential to seek the assistance of professionals. In these circumstances, the company secretary will probably act as the link with such professionals.

However, the regular and routine tasks of keeping the company books in order, and its records up to date, will inevitably fall to the company secretary. These relatively straightforward and routine tasks can adequately be dealt with by the company secretary, provided that he or she adopts a disciplined approach to the subject and follows a few basic rules of procedure. An organised and methodical approach not only makes the day-to-day administration simpler but also eases the changeover when a company secretary moves on to make way for another.

Most of the areas which fall within the functions of the company secretary have been identified earlier in this book. This chapter will take the company secretary through those areas where he or she can deal with matters with little or no outside assistance. Where there is doubt, use a professional, a solicitor, an accountant or perhaps the services of a member of the Institute of Chartered Secretaries.

Cost control is one of the main concerns in running a management company and it is possible at least to minimise large professional bills by carrying out the less complicated tasks oneself.

For the purpose of this overview, it has been assumed that either the original company formation has been handled by solicitors or that they have dealt with the takeover and transfer to the new regime.

Takeover　*

(A) FROM DIRECTORS WHO ARE NOT FLAT-OWNERS

In this case, the existing directors and company secretary will resign to permit the flat-owners to take over the existing company. New directors and company secretary will be appointed. The new appointments will need to be approved by the flat-owners who will become members of the management company at an EGM, although this may be done without the need for a meeting if a written resolution is approved by all members of the company and signed by them (see Chapter 8).

The company secretary will update the statutory books and file the appropriate forms at Companies House in respect of the resignation of the old officers, the appointment of the new officers and the creation of the new members of the company.

(B) WHERE A NEW MANAGEMENT COMPANY HAS BEEN FORMED

This is illustrated by the example of Flatco Limited in Chapter 4 where two flat-owners are the first officers of the company who then appoint further officers and cause the issue of the shares or memberships of the company.

(C) PREPARING FOR TAKEOVER

Much of this stage will have been set in place by the company's solicitors. Title to the property will have been transferred to the company (in most cases), insurance arrangements completed to coincide with the change of ownership, banking arrangements made and so on. The new company secretary will liaise either with the outgoing officers or the members to arrange a meeting to sanction the initial structure.

(D) THE ACTUAL TAKEOVER

When a meeting has been convened, the officers of the company are appointed. In Flatco Limited, for example, four directors are appointed, one having already been in place from formation. The company secretary resigns and a new appointment is made. Shares are then allotted to each flat-owner (if a share company) or membership certificates issued (if a guarantee company).

The new company secretary will take minutes of the meeting noting all the changes as a true record of proceedings and will, after takeover, be required to deal with all the other formalities (see **(E)** below).

In the case of the takeover from existing directors who are not flat-owners, the principles remain the same except that, in such cases, letters of resignation are produced from the outgoing officers and accepted by the meeting. New officers are then appointed and shares issued as before.

This first meeting may also carry out certain other business such as the authorisation of bank signatories or any other pressing matter relevant to the initial running of the company.

(E) AFTER TAKEOVER MEETING

The company secretary will prepare minutes of the meeting noting what went on. He or she will then update the statutory books, issue share certificates/membership certificates where appropriate and file all the forms which are required at Companies House (see below).

The company secretary will also probably hold the title deeds to the property and, in such cases, may wish to prepare a set of record cards which list the ownership of each property which can be updated when there is a change of ownership of a flat. Figure 1

(below) shows a suggested form of record which may be kept
either manually or, if required, on a computer database. (This latter
may be advisable if there are a large number of flats and it will
facilitate the sending of letters or demands to flat-owners when
necessary.)

Figure 1
Suggested form of deeds register

Address: Flat 1, Ingoldsby Mansions, Eastwick
Date of lease: 12.1.1981. Term of years: 999
Rent: £25 p.a. Date due: 1st January
Original parties: Bloggs & Co (1) Patrick Percival
                           (2) Current owner
(here note changes as they occur including date of change)
Notes:

CHECK-LIST

BEFORE TAKEOVER:

- confirm formation of company and transfer to company of
  property ownership (if applicable);
- receive deeds including counterpart leases from solicitors;
- arrange insurance cover for building;
- liaise with incoming directors;
- check bank arrangements including bank mandate forms if
  required;
- if takeover is of existing company, receive resignation letters
  from outgoing officers and share transfers and old certificates
  in respect of any shares held by them;
- decide upon company's accountants;
- decide upon location of company's registered office;

- obtain quotations for any anticipated management costs for first year;
- convene meeting.

AT TAKEOVER:

- note those attending;
- elect chairman;
- receive letters of resignation of outgoing officers (if applicable);
- appoint new directors and if necessary new company secretary;
- appoint new auditors/accountants (if necessary);
- confirm bank appointment;
- obtain signatures to bank mandate;
- agree change of registered office (if necessary);
- issue new shares/membership certificates;
- any other business.

AFTER TAKEOVER:

- prepare minutes of meeting;
- update statutory books;
- prepare and issue share certificates/membership certificates;
- file allotment notification (Form 88(2)) at Companies House if new shares have been issued (share companies only);
- file Form 288b in respect of the resignation and appointment of directors and company secretary;
- file Form 287 in respect of change of registered office;
- prepare deeds register;
- place deeds/statutory books in place of safe-keeping;
- return bank mandates to bank;
- carry out any other instructions issued at meeting.

Issuing shares (where company is limited by shares)   *

NOTE
It is likely that in most cases the company secretary will not need

to issue shares for the first time, since this will probably have been carried out by the developer's solicitor upon the sale of each flat by the developer. Sometimes, however, this may not have occurred and in such cases the procedures are as identified below.

In the case of the transfer of ownership of a flat, there will also be a transfer in ownership of the flat-owner's membership of the management company. This, where the company is limited by shares, is effected by way of a share transfer and the issue of a new share certificate.

CHECK-LIST

- When a new share is issued to a person, it is known as the allotment of a share. The price paid for each share is paid by the member to the company.
- When an existing share is transferred, this is done by means of a share transfer form. No new share is created, but simply the old share changes hands. The new owner pays the old owner the price for that share.
- Upon the allotment of a new share, the company secretary receives the payment and issues a share certificate to the new shareholder.
- Upon the transfer of an existing share, the company secretary receives the share transfer form from the new shareholder (or his solicitor) together with the old certificate. The old share certificate is then cancelled and a new share certificate issued to the new owner in place of the old. The certificate will be impressed with the company's seal and signed by a director and the company secretary. The transfer of ownership is registered in the membership register in the company's statutory books and details of the new shareholder entered.
- When a new share is allotted, the allotment must be notified to Companies House. The form detailing such allotments is Form 88(2) (see Appendix 1) and it must be filed within one month of such allotment.

- Upon a transfer of an existing share, no form needs to be filed at the time of transfer. The membership records will be updated at Companies House when the company secretary files the annual return each year. (Form 363a – see Appendix 1.)

Issuing membership certificates
(where company is limited by guarantee)

NOTE
The principle of membership of a company limited by guarantee is similar to that of a share company, the only difference being that there is no need to physically transfer a share. There is no share certificate evidencing membership of the company, merely a certificate of membership.

A membership certificate takes the place of a share certificate and is a record of a person's membership and their liability to be called upon for their contribution to the capital of the company.

CHECK-LIST

- New membership certificates are issued upon the application of a first flat-owner to become a member.
- Membership is transferred on change of ownership of a flat. Normally, no formal requirements are necessary other than notification of change of ownership. The old certificate is destroyed and a new certificate issued in the new owner's name.
- Since a guarantee company has no share capital, no Form 88(2) need be filed when a new member is admitted.

Dealing with change of flat-owner *

NOTE
When a flat-owner sells his or her property the transfer of ownership of the lease is known as an assignment.

With the transfer of the property the new flat-owner will become entitled to membership of the company. Most management companies within their Articles insist on this happening. They will also, normally, provide that if the flat-owner is also an officer of the company, then the outgoing flat-owner will be required to surrender this position on sale.

The solicitors who are acting for a new owner will ensure the transfer of membership of the management company alongside the assignment. They will inform the company secretary of the change of ownership and request the company secretary to update the company's records and issue new paperwork for the new flat-owner. There will usually be provisions in the lease for the payment of a small registration fee to the company for the registration.

CHECK-LIST

– Flat-owner completes purchase of flat by an assignment.
– New owner's solicitor obtains share transfer upon completion from the outgoing flat-owner's solicitors (if a share company) together with the old share certificate and if the old owner was an officer of the company his or her resignation from the post.
– The new owner's solicitor sends the following documents to the company secretary to permit the registration of the new flat-owner:

    (1) a notice of assignment in duplicate giving details of the new owner and the date of assignment and also details of any building society or lender who has taken a mortgage over the flat;

    (2) the share transfer form (stamped by the Inland Revenue with the appropriate stamp duty) (if share company);

    (3) the old share certificate (if share company);

    (4) the registration fee;

    (5) letter of resignation as director or company secretary and request for appointment (if applicable);

(6) request for membership of the company (if the company is limited by guarantee).

- Upon receipt, the company secretary acknowledges receipt of the notice of assignment by returning one receipted copy to the new owner's solicitors and banks the fee.
- The company secretary makes the appropriate entries in the registers of the statutory books, including the cancellation of the old share certificate (where applicable) and the issue of a new share certificate or membership certificate (if limited by guarantee).
- If there is a mortgage on the flat, it may be necessary to ensure that the lender's interest is noted on the building insurance policy.
- If the new flat-owner is to become a director, then the company secretary must file a Form 288a detailing his or her appointment and a Form 288b detailing the resignation of the outgoing director within 14 days of the change (see below) and also update the register of directors in the statutory books.
- The deeds register (if used) should be updated to show a record of the new owner of the flat.

Change of officers – Forms 288a, b and c

NOTE

Upon any change of director or company secretary, or where some personal detail of a company officer changes, these changes must be registered at Companies House on Form 288a, b or c (see Appendix 1). This form must be filed within 14 days of any change by the company secretary. One form is required to be filed for each individual change. There are explanatory notes on the form to assist completion.

When the form is received at the Registry, the records there will be updated and the changes will be reflected at the end of the year on the annual return. If any entries are incorrectly completed, the form will be returned to the person who filed it for correction and resubmission.

The contents of the forms are shown in Appendix 1.

Since the records held by Companies House should reflect the statutory books, the details sent for filing should, therefore, be entered, at the same time, by the company secretary in the statutory books.

The form must be signed by the company secretary or an active director of the company and dated before filing. There is an additional box for inclusion of an address to whom communications from Companies House will be directed.

The company secretary should retain a copy of each form filed with the statutory books for future reference.

Keeping minutes

NOTE
The company secretary should always record the proceedings of meetings, both of directors and shareholders/members. The way in which each company secretary takes such minutes is largely a matter of individual preference, but they should always be neatly written or, preferably, typed.

A copy of each set of minutes should be kept for reference. In the case of minutes of members' meetings, these should be kept with the statutory books, since they need to be available for inspection. The directors' minutes are usually kept in a separate folder.

The minutes should be signed by the chairman of the meeting as a true record. They will usually be presented for approval at the next meeting. In the case of general meetings (especially the AGM), the company secretary may care to circulate the minutes, prior to the next meeting, to the members to give them an opportunity to read them and to save time at the next meeting. A set of minutes of a typical AGM are included in Appendix 1.

As a matter of course, the minutes should record decisions made at the meetings and not be a verbatim transcript of everything that went on. Certain matters must be minuted as follows.

CHECK-LIST

– list of those attending;
– record of appointment of chairman;
– details of any resolutions passed.

Other forms sometimes encountered

Change of registered office – Form 287   *

This form is not often necessary for a flat management company where the building itself is usually the registered office. Sometimes, the registered office may be at the offices of the company's accountants and, in such cases, a change in accountants will necessitate a change in the registered office. This will frequently be handled by the new accountants. If not, the company secretary must complete this form and file it showing the new address.

NOTICE OF NEW ACCOUNTING REFERENCE DATE – FORM 225(1)(2)   ***

This form should always be dealt with by the company's accountants and is unlikely to be necessary in all but the most occasional circumstances.

REGISTRATION OF CHARGES – FORM 395   ***

It is unlikely that the company will mortgage its property. If it does, then this form must be filed to register the charge. It is usually dealt with by the lender's solicitors.

ANNUAL RETURN – FORM 363a (see below)

Contents of the statutory registers and books

Each of the sections of the statutory books is usually known as a folio and several folios will cross-refer with each other in the books. In addition to the registers, there are also two other parts of the statutory records, namely the certificate of incorporation and the Memorandum and Articles of Association, the originals of which should be kept with the statutory books.

The certificate of incorporation

This is the document issued by the Registrar of Companies when the company is formed (incorporated) and shows the company's name and number. It is, in effect, the document which proves the existence of the company and may need to be produced from time to time.

The Memorandum and Articles of Association

These have been referred to previously and represent the constitution and rules of the company. From time to time, some of the contents of these rules may need to be altered. If such action is contemplated, the company secretary is advised to seek professional help, since such alterations often require specialised procedures.

The statutory registers

NOTE
These comprise:

(1) register of applications and allotments of shares (share company only);
(2) register of transfer of shares (share company only);
(3) register of members;
(4) register of directors;
(5) register of company secretaries;
(6) register of directors' interests in shares;
(7) register of charges;
(8) register of sealings;
(9) minutes of meetings;
(10) blank share certificates/membership certificates;
(11) copies of documents lodged at Companies Registration Office.

CHECK-LIST

How to complete the registers

1. *Application and allotments of shares:*
-   only applicable if the company is a share company;
-   enter details of founder shareholders – only necessary in the case of a management company when the company is being set up. In such cases, each new flat-owner becomes a member at that time;
-   details of transfers of shares from the original shareholders will be entered in the transfer register;
-   when new allottees are entered, the details of the new shareholders must also be registered by filing Form 88(2) at Companies House.

(2) *Register of transfers of shares:*
-   only applicable if the company is a share company;

- enter details of change of ownership and date of change and name of new owner (*see* Dealing with change of flat-owner at p 101). Cross-refer to folio in allotment register if transfer from original shareholder;
- need not be registered at Companies House until annual return is filed at the end of the year (see below);
- when a new entry is made, the new owner will be issued with a new share certificate drawn from the blank certificates contained in the register.

(3) *Register of members:*
- keep up to date when a new member is admitted (share company or guarantee company);
- each folio gives full details of the name, address, and number of shares (if a share company) held by the member;
- give date of becoming a member and when the member changes, insert the date of transfer from the transfer register. Do not remove details of retiring member so as to keep a continuous record of share ownership.

(4) *Register of directors:*
- keep a separate record of each director;
- enter all details on the register, mirroring the information which must be entered on Form 288a, b or c (*see* Change of officers – Forms 228a, b and c at p 103);
- insert date of appointment and resignation when the director leaves;
- on each change, the register will reflect the changes included in Form 288a, b or c filed at Companies House.

(5) *Register of company secretaries:*
- as with the register of directors, this must be updated with the records of the incoming company secretary on each change (Form 288a, b or c must be filed).

(6) *Register of directors' interests:*
- any director of the company must have details inserted of his shareholding in the company in this register.

(7) *Register of charges:*
- in most management companies, this register will not be necessary;

–   if there is any mortgage over the management company's legal
     title to the building, then this must be entered in this register
     and the appropriate Form 395 filed at Companies House (seek
     professional assistance).

(8) *Register of sealings:*
–   each time the company seal is used on formal documents (eg
     share certificates) the details of the date of sealing and the
     nature of the document should be entered on this register.

(9) *Minutes:*
–   the minutes of general meetings should be kept with the
     books, either in the main books or as a separate minute book
     as a record of proceedings of the company.

(10) *Blank share certificates/membership certificates:*
–   kept with the books for use on the issue of new certificates to
     incoming members;
–   upon issue, insert all relevant details and apply seal. Ensure
     that the certificate is appropriately signed by authorised
     officers (director and company secretary) before issue. Write
     details of share certificate on detachable counterfoil. Ensure
     the details are entered in the register of sealings.

(11) *Copies of documents lodged at Companies House:*
–   only kept as a matter of record;
–   it is useful to retain copies of all forms which have been filed
     with the books for reference by future officers of the
     company so that they can familiarise themselves with the
     current structure of the company.

FILING ANNUAL ACCOUNTS AND ANNUAL RETURN **

Annual accounts

Despite being a non-trading company, a flat management company
is still obliged to lay its accounts and deliver them to Companies
House annually. The company's accountants will usually see to this
requirement.

Failure to file accounts on time will give rise to fines and other consequences, causing the company problems with striking off (see Chapter 11).

The company will have what is known as an 'accounting reference date' being a date notified to Companies House as the date up to which the annual accounts will be drawn each year. (This may be changed in certain circumstances – take professional advice.)

The time in which the accounts must be filed is no later than 10 months after the relevant accounting reference period. There are certain variations for filing where the first accounting period is concerned or where an accounting reference period has changed. (This should be dealt with by the company's accountants.)

New accounting reference dates are notified to Companies House using Form 225.

With small companies such as management companies the contents of the accounts can be simplified and the company's accountants will be aware of these provisions when drawing up the accounts.

Companies House will send out an annual reminder when accounts are due and this should not be ignored.

Annual return

The annual return is filed annually at Companies House along with the appropriate fee. It is an important document which allows the updating of changes since the date of the last annual return. Certain matters, such as change of shareholders or members, have previously been highlighted.

Failure to complete and submit an annual return can have disastrous consequences for the company such as leading it to be struck off (see Chapter 11).

When to file the return

The return must be filed on the anniversary of the previous return ('the return date') or, in the case of a newly incorporated company, on the anniversary of its date of incorporation (stated on the certificate of incorporation – see above).

Contents of return

Certain information regarding share capital is required. Originally, there were many details which had to be inserted which have been much simplified. Details of the type of company and its principal business activities must be inserted in the appropriate boxes. Details are also inserted of the company's officers.

The company's professional advisers will be able to assist the officers of the company to take advantage of new 'elective resolutions' which permit the dispensing with the holding of an AGM and the laying of accounts before a general meeting.

If this course of action is to be adopted, then the return should state this fact.

It is felt that it would be inappropriate for a flat management company to adopt this procedure in view of the necessity of giving flat-owners at least one chance each year to call the officers of the company to account for their actions on the members' behalf.

Simplification in future form-filling

Once the computer at Companies House has the full information of the present state of the company, future forms will automatically be generated annually on the anniversary of the previous return, and sent to the company at its registered office.

The Form 363s is a 'shuttle' form, containing in it, preprinted, all those details which appeared on the previous form which was filed the previous year. It is a simple matter for the company secretary to compare the information shown on the return and detail any changes which have occurred which are not shown on the return and then return the amended form so that the computerised records may be updated.

Ensuring receipt of annual return

Many company secretaries overlook the annual return because it is sent to the registered office which is at an address other than the company secretary's own address. This may be, for instance, the address of a professional adviser. In such cases, it is wise to diarise the anniversary of the annual return and ensure that the form is forwarded as soon as received. It is all too easy to forget this important requirement and find out too late that the company has been struck off. The consequent difficulties involved are outlined in Chapter 11.

Company Stationery – the Statutory Requirements

COMPANY NAME

The full company name, ie the name on the company's certificate of incorporation, *must* be shown in legible characters on all:

- business letters;
- notices and official publications;
- bills of exchange, promissory notes, endorsements, cheques, orders for money or goods;
- bills of parcels, invoices, receipts, letters of credit.

Failure to comply causes the company and its officers and any person who issued the incorrect document to be liable to a fine. Any officer or other person who signs a cheque, order for money or goods, bill of exchange, promissory note or endorsement which does not show the company name correctly can be personally liable for the amount of the cheque etc.

OTHER DETAILS REQUIRED

All business letters and order forms must also show:

- the address of the registered office;
- the place of registration (England and Wales or Scotland);
- the registered number of the company.

There is no need to give details of share capital on letters or order forms. However, if any reference to share capital is included, it must be to paid-up share capital only.

If these requirements are not observed, the company and its officers and any person who issues an incorrect letter or order will be liable to a fine.

DIRECTORS' DETAILS

It is not necessary to show any details of directors on company stationery. However, if any of the directors' details are shown, the following information must be given for every director:

- individuals – present Christian name or forename (or initials) and surname;
- companies – full corporate name (ie as on the certificate of incorporation).

Failure to comply causes the company and its officers to be liable to a fine.

BUSINESS NAMES

If a company operates under any name other than its true corporate name (ie the name on its certificate of incorporation), it must state its true name on all business letters, orders for goods or services, invoices, receipts and written demands for payment of debts. Any person who fails to comply with this requirement is liable to a fine.

hapter **Eleven**
When Things go Wrong

Introduction

Provided that the preceding rules and procedures are followed, there is no reason why there should be any difficulties in running a flat management company, but even in the best run company, at some time, a problem may arise.

Many of the problems associated with running any form of company have been highlighted in previous chapters. Ignorance of the statutory requirements of running a company of any sort, from filing forms to maintaining proper accounts, is no excuse and there are penalties on directors for such failure. Companies House advertise this fact in newspapers pointing out that, not only are there fines, but certain failures can result in a criminal record. Just because the company is a vehicle for administration of a property, does not make it different from any other limited company, and understanding of this will go a long way to ensure that the director of a flat management company takes his or her responsibilities seriously.

Of course, it is not always formal requirements which can be the cause of problems. The company will consist of a wide variety of individuals, each with his or her own point to make or prove. The politics of running the company would make a book in their own right. The only word of advice in respect of such problems is to learn the art of man management, the politician's art, and be prepared for criticism, the searching question, and the hostile flat-owner. The disciplines imposed by the actual formalities of the company itself can assist in limiting the political problems but they will always be there waiting to trap the unwary director who takes it upon him- or herself to exceed the specific brief given.

Sanctions for failure to comply with legal requirements

The ultimate sanction is the loss of the company itself – 'striking-off'. This occurs when Companies House fails to be provided with the appropriate statutory information, usually the annual return and the accounts. This Draconian measure has always been a thorn in the side of management companies where there are frequent changes in personnel, leading to a lack of continuity in the management and control of the company. The process of restoring the company can be long and expensive.

Fortunately, with the era of computerisation and the introduction of the new regime, outlined in Chapter 10, of standard computerised annual returns, the days when companies were regularly struck off for failure to file these returns may be coming to an end. However, it is still possible to ignore reminders sent out by Companies House.

There should be a simple rule – attend to such reminders as soon as they are received and then they will not be left until it is too late.

A company can also be wound up if it cannot pay its debts. This should not happen in the case of a flat management company. 'Winding-up' is the term by which a company is put into liquidation. It contrasts with 'striking-off' in that the latter is instituted by Companies House, whereas the former is normally instituted by creditors of the company.

If for some reason a flat management company is wound up, that fact can sometimes lead to personal liability falling on its directors for the company's debts (seek professional advice).

There is no reason at all why a management company should be wound up, since it is not trading and its income should match its expenditure. If a management company fails to collect its income, then it may not be able to meet its commitments in this regard and it is therefore possible for it to be wound up.

The best way of avoiding this is to take action to ensure that income is paid when due. There is no excuse for a management company to be wound up by outside creditors.

Directors' penalties ***

It is now important to remember that as a director, a flat-owner is liable to penalties both financial and otherwise.

Failure to file an annual return or completing it improperly may result in a fine of up to £5,000 and there may also be daily default fines. There are also other fines for other defaults specified in the Companies Act.

Directors may also be disqualified from acting as a director in certain cases where there is persistent default in submitting documents.

The simplest way to ensure that none of these occur is to apply basic procedures and observe good discipline. Failures to observe these matters in respect of a relatively insignificant management company may well seriously affect a flat-owner's position, say, as director of another larger trading company.

Points to watch

Good discipline and remembering basic procedures will make the necessity to read this chapter unnecessary. Reference to this chapter will probably mean that an officer of the company has not performed his functions correctly.

The following is a check-list of those items which should always be uppermost in a director or company secretary's mind:

(1)   file changes of details of officers within 14 days of change;

(2)   keep the statutory books up to date at all times;

(3)   ensure statutory accounts are prepared within the time-limits set, namely 10 months from the end of the accounting period;

(4)   file annual returns on time;

(5)   diarise critical dates for dealing with important company matters;

(6)   have good professional advisers at hand when necessary and, if in doubt, consult them before taking any action on company matters;

(7)   keep all flat-owners informed of any major item of importance as to the well-being of the collective group or a particular individual;

(8)   if things do go wrong, then do not wait until it is too late before acting;

(9)   keep legal documents such as leases and the other title documents in a secure place, and refer to the leases when questions arise about them;

(10) understand the provisions of the leases so that service charges are recoverable in respect of the items of expenditure incurred;

(11) do not permit individual flat-owners to delay payment of monies owing by them for too long and, if necessary, enforce payments by appropriate action.

Striking-off – the ultimate sanction?   ***

What if the company is struck off the register? It is a common occurrence for a company secretary to attempt to file some document at Companies House only to receive a brief note from the Registrar of Companies informing him or her that the form has not been accepted owing to the fact that the company has ceased to exist. Panic is often the first reaction, since the company has ceased to exist and, as such, cannot act in any legal capacity whatsoever.

CONSEQUENCES OF STRIKING-OFF

Striking-off of any company will not have occurred without several warning letters having been sent to the company notifying it of the Registrar's intention to strike it off the register if certain matters are not rectified within certain time-limits.

When the notice periods have been exhausted, the Registrar removes the company from the roll of companies and advertises this fact in the *London Gazette* (or the *Edinburgh Gazette* in the case of companies registered in Scotland).

From that moment, the company ceases to exist, and all assets of the company become the property of the Crown. In the case of a management company, this will mean that the building of which each flat-owner owns a part will not longer be owned by their flat management company, since it itself no longer exists.

As it has ceased to exist, the company, as a separate legal person, has no legal capacity whatsoever and, consequently, cannot enter into any legal agreement with others and cannot act as the manager of the building. The Crown becomes the flat-owners' landlord and control passes from the flat-owners to the Crown.

ACTIONS UPON DISCOVERY OF STRIKING-OFF

The company may well have continued to act as a company, ignorant of the fact that it had been struck off. When the fact of striking-off has been brought to the attention of the officers of the defunct company, the first action should be to consult with the company's legal advisers. There will then begin the process of its restoration. The company may be restored at any time within 20 years of being struck off (subject to certain exceptions) and if and when it is restored the company will be treated as if it had never been struck off and all actions carried out by it in the period following striking-off will be revalidated.

RESTORATION PROCEDURES   * * *

The formal application to restore a company should **always** be handled by a solicitor, since it is important that certain formalities are strictly adhered to.

It is not proposed to detail all these procedures in this book, but simply to give an understanding of just how advisable it is to prevent striking-off from happening in the first place.

Application is made through the courts to the Registrar of Companies and its representative, the Treasury Solicitor, for restoration. Such application is made in the first instance by one of the members of the company at the time of striking-off. That member prepares a sworn statement (an affidavit) setting out the circumstances which led to the company being struck off and requesting the court to order the company's restoration. That member also undertakes to the court to ensure that all matters outstanding which had been the cause of the striking-off are dealt with and brought up to date so that when the company returns to the roll its affairs will be in order.

The Treasury Solicitor considers the application on behalf of the Registrar of Companies and requests that before the company is restored, certain matters are rectified so that at the date at which the order is given for restoration, all outstanding deficiencies in the statutory records are corrected. This procedure may take some time, and in the case of companies which may have been struck off for some time, may require the production of annual accounts for all the outstanding years.

When all these requirements have been complied with, the Treasury Solicitor will signify that he is now happy that restoration may take place. An order will be agreed, which is then presented at a hearing at court. The company will then be ordered to be restored to the roll of companies and the Registrar, upon receipt of a copy of the order, will re-enter the company's name on the roll and advertise this fact in the *London Gazette* or *Edinburgh Gazette* (as appropriate).

One final point relates to the costs involved in this procedure. Not only will the company, newly restored, have to pay the professional fees of its own solicitor and, perhaps, its accountant, but also the costs of the Registrar of Companies and the Treasury Solicitor.

Summary

- Avoid striking-off. It is unnecessary and costly.
- Simple disciplines, if adopted, will help to prevent it occurring.
- Follow standard procedures and do not ignore correspondence received from Companies House.
- If striking-off does occur, then upon discovering the fact, act fast to restore the company.
- Use a solicitor to make the application to restore.

- The procedure can take some months to complete depending on how much needs to be filed to bring the company back up to date. If successful, the company is restored to its former state and, with care, the same problem should not arise again.

hapter **Twelve**
Seeking Professional Assistance

Introduction

Many aspects of a procedural nature and the practical problems of running a flat management company can quite easily be dealt with by the officers of the company provided that a disciplined approach is adopted. Inevitably, however, there will be occasions when it will be necessary to consult and obtain assistance from professional advisers.

Some flat management companies may find within the ranks of their flat-owners, people who are able to give professional advice, such as solicitors and accountants. It is certainly useful to have such flat-owners, since advice given by them may well be given at no cost.

By using professionals to advise, the management company will often save time and expense in the long run. A solicitor will be able to deal with a particular legal problem, for instance, quickly, and with the minimum of investigation, whereas a lay person may eventually find the right solution but only after hours of research. It therefore makes sense to ensure the use of such services if there is any doubt about how to proceed.

Fees

The use of professionals, be they solicitors, accountants or others, will involve cost, and for the flat management company, cost is a critical item. Such services will not be paid out of trading profits, but out of the pockets of the flat-owners themselves.

It is an expense which can be ascertained, in general, before it is incurred, and most professionals will, if asked, provide a guide on the cost of carrying out such work before it begins.

There is often an economic benefit in using such services, since if matters are dealt with wrongly by an officer of the company, it is quite likely that the resulting costs of rectifying any mistakes could be much higher in the long run.

When to use professionals

Of the many types of professional adviser, the most important will be the company's accountant. It is the accountant whose services are required at least once a year to prepare the annual accounts and audit them. Since this is a statutory requirement, it is a cost which cannot be avoided.

Accountants

The extent of involvement of the company's accountants depends on the size of the flat management company. Larger companies may need a regular bookkeeping service from their accountants and the preparation of management accounts. Smaller companies will probably need accountants only for the production of the annual accounts.

WHEN TO USE ACCOUNTANTS

The services of accountants should be used as follows.
(1) When starting the company, to advise:

- in the setting up of accounting procedures;
- the preparation of service charge estimates;
- the format of the company's accounting records;
- if necessary, in assisting in obtaining finance.

(2) Each year:

- to provide continuing advice on cost estimates for the coming year;
- to assist in the preparation of management accounts;
- to discuss improvements to the method by which accounting records are kept;
- to prepare and/or audit the annual statutory accounts of the company;
- to advise on matters that may arise in the accounts.

HOW TO CHOOSE AN ACCOUNTANT

Cost is an important consideration in making a choice of accountant, but equally important will be the ability of the accountant to handle the job. It is a good idea to choose a local accountant, since it saves the cost of him travelling long distances to prepare the accounts. An accountant may be found by recommendation or even, as a last resort, from the Yellow Pages.

The size of the management company itself may have a bearing on who is chosen. There is little point in using the service of a large multi-national accountancy firm when the company is small; the overheads of such a firm will undoubtedly make their use uneconomical.

The accountant must be suitably qualified (either chartered or certified), and should be able to audit the accounts as well.

Solicitors

The solicitor's role is important to a management company, since the company is property-based and, as such, there will often be questions of interpretation to be made in respect of the leases, and it will have been necessary, on taking over the building, for the solicitor to check the title to the building.

WHEN TO USE SOLICITORS

(1) When starting the company, the solicitor will be involved as follows:

-   forming the company, issuing shares, changing the name of the company (if required). (Note: this service can also be provided by accountants);
-   advising on the acquisition of the building, including advice on the best method of legal ownership, checking title to the building, transferring ownership to the management company;

- preparing the statutory registers before handing them over to the new company secretary;
- advising on the provisions contained in the leases of the flats;
- identifying any discrepancies in the leases which require amendment and dealing with same on behalf of the company.

(2) Day-to-day involvement by solicitors might be required for the following:

- advising on specific legal problems as and when they occur;
- preparing and filing statutory forms on behalf of the company secretary;
- assisting in completion of statutory forms;
- assisting in collection of rent and service charges from recalcitrant flat-owners;
- advising and dealing with restoration of the company in the event that it is struck off.

Surveyors

Large flat management companies will often require the assistance of a firm of chartered surveyors who will manage the common parts of the building on the company's behalf for a set fee. This will free the officers of the company from the day-to-day problems of hiring contractors, getting repair work carried out and even in preparing any service charge demands.

The choice of surveyor is again a matter of personal choice, but it is advisable to select a firm which is local with good knowledge of the area and the contractors available in the area.

Quantity surveyors may sometimes be required to prepare specifications of major maintenance work which may from time to time need to be carried out. This will be on a one-off basis for a particular matter.

Architects

The management company may, occasionally, need to use the services of a firm of architects on works to be carried out to the building and to prepare plans, obtain planning permission (if required) and to supervise the carrying out of such works.

The fees for such services should be agreed before any work is carried out.

Company secretarial services

Some companies may use the services of a professional company secretary.

Bank managers

The choice of bank manager is made by the officers of the company and will again be a personal choice. In general, since the company is unlikely to require anything but the usual bank account facilities, most major banks will be suitable. If money is to be held on deposit, then consideration may be given to favouring a bank which offers the most competitive rates of interest on its deposit accounts. It may be that a building society will be chosen in preference to a bank, if its deposit rates are better.

Summary

- Avoid the pitfalls of going it alone. The use of professional advisers will help to guide the management company to comply with all formal requirements.
- Identify those areas where specific professional help is necessary, and appoint professionals at an early stage.
- Agree fees with professionals used before any work is carried out. Where such fees are substantial, obtain the agreement of all flat-owners to such expenditure, in advance.
- If things go wrong, then seek professional advice as soon as possible to rectify any mistakes.

ppendix **One**
Useful Forms

Statutory Registers

Forms for Filing

Memorandum and Articles of Association

AGM

Service Charges

Form 1: Register of Applications and Allotments (share company only)

Register of Applications and Allotments

Class of Shares _____

Entry No.	Date of Application	Date of Allotment	Name of Applicant	Number of shares		Price per share	Amount paid	Allotted for consideration other than cash	Number of		Entered in Register of Members	Remarks
				Applied for	Allotted				Allotment Letter	Share Certificate		

Form 2: Register of Transfers (share company only)

Form 2: Register of Transfers (share company only)

Register of Transfers

Transfer No.	Date of Registration	Transferee						Transferor					
		Name	No. of shares acquired	Price or consideration	No. of Share Certificate	Sealing Register reference		Name	No. of shares for which certificate surrendered	Balance Certificate		Sealing Register reference
										No. of shares	Certificate no.	

Form 3: Register of Members (share company)

Register of Members (share company)

Name
Address
Dividends to

Class of share
Denomination
Date of entry as member
Date of cessation of membership

Date of Allotment OR Entry of Transfer	References in Register		No. of Share Certificate	Amount paid or agreed to be considered as paid	Acquisitions	Disposals	Balance	Remarks
	Allotments	Transfers						

Form 4: Register of Members (guarantee company)

Form 4: Register of Members (guarantee company)

Register of Members

Number of Membership Certificate

Surname

Forename(s)

Address

Date of Entry as a Member:

Date of Ceasing to be a Member:

REMARKS:

Signature of Member:

Date:

Number of Membership Certificate

Surname

Forename(s)

Address

Date of Entry as a Member:

Date of Ceasing to be a Member:

REMARKS:

Signature of Member:

Date:

Form 5: Register of Directors

Register of Directors

	Other Directorships	Date of resignation

Surname _(or Corporate Name if appropriate)_

Forename(s)

Any former Forenames or Surnames

Residential Address _(or Registered or Principal Office if appropriate)_

Nationality

Date of Birth

Business Occupation

DATES OF:

Appointment — Resignation or Cessation

Minute — Minute

Filing Particulars — Filing Particulars

Form 6: Register of Secretaries

Form 6: Register of Secretaries

Register of Secretaries

Surname _____
(or Corporate Name if appropriate)

Forename(s) _____

Any former Forenames or Surnames _____

Residential Address _____
(or Registered or Principal Office if appropriate)
_____
_____
_____

DATES OF:

Appointment	Resignation or Cessation
_____	_____
Minute	Minute
_____	_____
Filing Particulars	Filing Particulars

Surname _____
(or Corporate Name if appropriate)

Forename(s) _____

Any former Forenames or Surnames _____

Residential Address _____
(or Registered or Principal Office if appropriate)
_____
_____
_____

DATES OF:

Appointment	Resignation or Cessation
_____	_____
Minute	Minute
_____	_____
Filing Particulars	Filing Particulars

Form 7: 363a Annual Return

Please complete in typescript,
or in bold black capitals.

CHFP001

363a

Annual Return

Company Number |

Company Name in full |
|

	Day	Month	Year

Date of this return
The information in this return is made up to

⌞ ⌞ / ⌞ ⌞ / ⌞ ⌞ ⌞ ⌞

Date of next return
If you wish to make your next return
to a date earlier than the anniversary
of this return please show the date here.
Companies House will then send a form
at the appropriate time.

Day   Month   Year

⌞ ⌞ / ⌞ ⌞ / ⌞ ⌞ ⌞ ⌞

Registered Office
Show here the address **at the date of**
this return.

|

|

Any change of   Post town
registered office
must *be notified*   County / Region
on form 287.

|

|

UK Postcode   ⌞ ⌞ ⌞ ⌞   ⌞ ⌞ ⌞

Principal business activities

Show trade classification code number(s)
for the principal activity or activities.

|_____| |_____|

|_____| |_____|

If the code number cannot be determined,
give a brief description of principal activity.

|

|

| Companies House receipt date barcode | When you have completed and signed the form please send it to the Registrar of Companies at: **Companies House, Crown Way, Cardiff, CF14 3UZ   DX 33050 Cardiff** for companies registered in England and Wales or |

Form revised September 1999

Companies House, 37 Castle Terrace, Edinburgh, EH1 2EB
for companies registered in Scotland   **DX 235 Edinburgh**

CHAD 21/12/99

Page 1

Form 7: 363a Annual Return

Register of members

If the register of members is not kept at the registered office, state here where it is kept.

Post town

County / Region

UK Postcode ⌞ ⌞ ⌞ ⌞   ⌞ ⌞ ⌞

Register of Debenture holders

If there is a register of debenture holders, or a duplicate of any such register or part of it, which is not kept at the registered office, state here where it is kept.

Post town

County / Region

UK Postcode ⌞ ⌞ ⌞ ⌞   ⌞ ⌞ ⌞

Company type

Public limited company ☐

Private company limited by shares ☐

Private company limited by guarantee without share capital ☐

Private company limited by shares exempt under section 30 ☐

Private company limited by guarantee exempt under section 30 ☐

Private unlimited company with share capital ☐

Private unlimited company without share capital ☐

Please tick the appropriate box

Company Secretary

Details of a new company secretary must be notified on form 288a.

(Please photocopy this area to provide details of joint secretaries).

* Voluntary details.

If a partnership give the names and addresses of the partners or the name of the partnership and office address.

Usual residential address must be given. In the case of a corporation or a Scottish firm, give the registered or principal office address.

Name

* Style / Title

Forename(s)

Surname

Address

Post town

County / Region

UK Postcode ⌞ ⌞ ⌞ ⌞   ⌞ ⌞ ⌞

Country

Directors

Please list directors in alphabetical order.

Details of new directors must be notified on form 288a

Name	* Style / Title

_____

Directors In the case of a director that is a corporation or a Scottish firm, the name is the corporate or firm name.

Day   Month   Year

Date of birth   └─└─/└─└─/└─└─└─└─

Forename(s) |_____

Surname |_____

Address |_____

Usual residential address must be given. In the case of a corporation or a Scottish firm, give the registered or principal office address.

|_____

Post town |_____

County / Region |_____   UK Postcode └─└─└─└─ └─└─└─

Country |_____   **Nationality** |_____

Business occupation |_____

* Voluntary details.

Name	* Style / Title

_____

Directors In the case of a director that is a corporation or a Scottish firm, the name is the corporate or firm name.

Day   Month   Year

Date of birth   └─└─/└─└─/└─└─└─└─

Forename(s) |_____

Surname |_____

Address |_____

Usual residential address must be given. In the case of a corporation or a Scottish firm, give the registered or principal office address.

|_____

Post town |_____

County / Region |_____   UK Postcode └─└─└─└─ └─└─└─

Country |_____   **Nationality** |_____

Business occupation |_____

CHAD 21/12/99

Page 3

Form 7: 363a Annual Return

Issued share capital
Enter details of all the shares in issue
at the date of this return.

Class *(e.g. Ordinary/Preference)*	Number of shares issued	Aggregate Nominal Value *(i.e Number of shares issued multiplied by nominal value per share, or total amount of stock)*
L_____	L_____	L_____
L_____	L_____	L_____
L_____	L_____	L_____
L_____	L_____	L_____
Totals	L_____	L_____

List of past and present shareholders
(Use attached schedule where appropriate)
A full list is required if one was not
included with either of the last two
returns.

There were no changes in the period [ ]

	on paper	in another format
A list of changes is enclosed	[ ]	[ ]
A full list of shareholders is enclosed	[ ]	[ ]

Certificate

I certify that the information given in this return is true to the best of my
knowledge and belief.

Signed [_____]   **Date** [_____]

† Please delete as appropriate

† a director / secretary

When you have signed the return send it
with the fee to the Registrar of Companies.
Cheques should be made payable to
Companies House.

This return includes [_____] continuation sheets.

(enter number)

Please give the name, address,
telephone number, and if available,
a DX number and Exchange, for
the person Companies House should
contact if there is any query.

L_____

L_____

L_____ Tel L_____

DX number L_____ DX exchange L_____

Directors

Please list directors in alphabetical order.

Details of new directors must be notified on form 288a

Name　　* Style / Title

Directors　In the case of a director that is a corporation or a Scottish firm, the name is the corporate or firm name.

Date of birth

Day　　Month　　　Year

Forename(s)

Surname

Address

Usual residential address must be given. In the case of a corporation or a Scottish firm, give the registered or principal office address.

Post town

County / Region　　　　　　　　　　UK Postcode

Country　　　　　　　**Nationality**

Business occupation

* Voluntary details.

Name　　* Style / Title

Directors　In the case of a director that is a corporation or a Scottish firm, the name is the corporate or firm name.

Date of birth

Day　　Month　　　Year

Forename(s)

Surname

Address

Usual residential address must be given. In the case of a corporation or a Scottish firm, give the registered or principal office address.

Post town

County / Region　　　　　　　　　　UK Postcode

Country　　　　　　　**Nationality**

Business occupation

Form 7: 363a Annual Return

Directors

Details of new directors must be notified on form 288a

Please list directors in alphabetical order.

Name   * Style / Title

Directors In the case of a director that is a corporation or a Scottish firm, the name is the corporate or firm name.

Date of birth   Day   Month   Year

L L / L L / L L L L

Forename(s)

Surname

Address

Usual residential address must be given. In the case of a corporation or a Scottish firm, give the registered or principal office address.

Post town

County / Region   UK Postcode   L L L L   L L L

Country   **Nationality**

Business occupation

* Voluntary details.

Name   * Style / Title

Directors In the case of a director that is a corporation or a Scottish firm, the name is the corporate or firm name.

Date of birth   Day   Month   Year

L L / L L / L L L L

Forename(s)

Surname

Address

Usual residential address must be given. In the case of a corporation or a Scottish firm, give the registered or principal office address.

Post town

County / Region   UK Postcode   L L L L   L L L

Country   **Nationality**

Business occupation

List of past and present shareholders
Schedule to form 363a

Company Number

Company Name in full

➤ Changes to shareholders particulars or details of the amount of stock or shares transferred must be completed each year
➤ You must provide a "full list" of all the company shareholders on:
- The company's first annual return following incorporation;
- Every third annual return after a full list has been provided
➤ List the company shareholders in alphabetical order or provide an index
➤ List joint shareholders consecutively

Shareholders' details	Class and number of shares or amount of stock held	Shares or amount of stock transferred *(if appropriate)*	
		Class and number of shares or amount of stock transferred	Date of registration of transfer
Name Address UK Postcode ⌐ ⌐ ⌐ ⌐ ⌐ ⌐ ⌐			
Name Address UK Postcode ⌐ ⌐ ⌐ ⌐ ⌐ ⌐ ⌐			
Name Address UK Postcode ⌐ ⌐ ⌐ ⌐ ⌐ ⌐ ⌐			

CHAD 21/12/99

Form 7: 363a Annual Return

List of past and present shareholders (Continued)

Company Number _____

Shareholders' details	Class and number of shares or amount of stock held	Shares or amount of stock transferred *(if appropriate)*	
		Class and number of shares or amount of stock transferred	Date of registration of transfer
Name L-------------------------------------- **Address** L-------------------------------------- L-------------------------------------- L-------------------------------------- **UK Postcode** L L L L L L L			
Name L-------------------------------------- **Address** L-------------------------------------- L-------------------------------------- L-------------------------------------- **UK Postcode** L L L L L L L			
Name L-------------------------------------- **Address** L-------------------------------------- L-------------------------------------- L-------------------------------------- **UK Postcode** L L L L L L L			
Name L-------------------------------------- **Address** L-------------------------------------- L-------------------------------------- L-------------------------------------- **UK Postcode** L L L L L L L			
Name L-------------------------------------- **Address** L-------------------------------------- I-------------------------------------- L-------------------------------------- **UK Postcode** L L L L L L L			

CHAD 21/12/99

Form 8: 288a Appointment of director or secretary

JORDANS

Please complete in typescript, or in bold black capitals.
CHFP001

288a

APPOINTMENT of director or secretary
(NOT for resignation (use Form 288b) or change of particulars (use Form 288c))

Company Number

Company Name in full

Appointment form

Notes on completion appear on reverse.

	Day	Month	Year		†Date of Birth	Day	Month	Year

Date of appointment

Appointment as director | as secretary

Please mark the appropriate box. If appointment is as a director and secretary mark both boxes.

NAME

*Style / Title — *Honours etc

Forename(s)

Surname

Previous Forename(s) — Previous Surname(s)

Usual residential address

Post town — Postcode

County / Region — Country

†Nationality — †Business occupation

†Other directorships (additional space overleaf)

I consent to act as ** director / secretary of the above named company

Consent signature — Date

* Voluntary details.
† Directors only.
** Delete as appropriate

A director, secretary etc must sign the form below.

Signed — Date

(**a director / secretary / administrator / administrative receiver / receiver manager / receiver)

Please give the name, address, telephone number and, if available, a DX number and Exchange of the person Companies House should contact if there is any query

Tel

DX number — DX exchange

Companies House receipt date barcode

When you have completed and signed the form please send it to the Registrar of Companies at:
Companies House, Crown Way, Cardiff, CF14 3UZ DX 33050 Cardiff
for companies registered in England and Wales   or
Companies House, 37 Castle Terrace, Edinburgh, EH1 2EB
for companies registered in Scotland   **DX 235 Edinburgh**

Form revised July 1998

JFL0009A / Rev 5.6   10/99

Form 8: 288a Appointment of director or secretary

Company Number

† Directors only.   †Other directorships

NOTES

Show the full forenames, NOT INITIALS. If the director or secretary is a corporation or Scottish firm, show the name on surname line and registered or principal office on the usual residential line.

Give previous forenames or surname(s) except:
- for a married woman, the name by which she was known before marriage need not be given.
- for names not used since the age of 18 or for at least 20 years.
A peer or individual known by a title may state the title instead of or in addition to the forenames and surname and need not give the name by which that person was known before he or she adopted the title or succeeded to it.

Other directorships.

Give the name of every company incorporated in Great Britain of which the person concerned is a director or has been a director at any time in the past five years.

You may exclude a company which either is, or at all times during the past five years when the person concerned was a director, was
- dormant
- a parent company which wholly owned the company making the return, or
- another wholly owned subsidiary of the same parent company.

JFL0009B / Rev 5.6   10/99

Form 9: 288b Terminating appointment as director or secretary

JORDANS

288b

Please complete in typescript, or in bold black capitals.

CHFP001

Terminating appointment as director or secretary
(NOT for appointment (use Form 288a) or change of particulars (use Form 288c))

Company Number

Company Name in full

	Day	Month	Year

Date of termination of appointment

as director   **as secretary**   *Please mark the appropriate box. If terminating appointment as a director and secretary mark both boxes.*

NAME   *Style / Title*   *Honours etc*

Please insert details as previously notified to Companies House.

Forename(s)

Surname

	Day	Month	Year

†Date of Birth

A serving director, secretary etc must sign the form below.

Signed   **Date**

* Voluntary details.
† Directors only.
**Delete as appropriate

(**serving director / secretary / administrator / administrative receiver / receiver manager / receiver)

Please give the name, address, telephone number and, if available, a DX number and Exchange of the person Companies House should contact if there is any query,

Tel

DX number   **DX exchange**

Companies House receipt date barcode

When you have completed and signed the form please send it to the Registrar of Companies at:
Companies House, Crown Way, Cardiff, CF14 3UZ   DX 33050 Cardiff
for companies registered in England and Wales   **or**
Companies House, 37 Castle Terrace, Edinburgh, EH1 2EB
for companies registered in Scotland   **DX 235 Edinburgh**

Form revised 1999

10/99

Form 10: 288c Change of particulars for director or secretary

IJ
JORDANS

Please complete in typescript, or in bold black capitals.
CHFP001

288c

CHANGE OF PARTICULARS for director or secretary *(NOT for appointment (use Form 288a) or resignation (use Form 288b))*

Company Number [ ]

Company Name in full [ ]

Changes of particulars form — *Complete in all cases*

Date of change of particulars [Day Month Year]

Name
Style / Title [ ] *Honours etc* [ ]
Forename(s) [ ]
Surname [ ]

†Date of Birth [Day Month Year]

Change of name *(enter new name)*
Forename(s) [ ]
Surname [ ]

Change of usual residential address
(enter new address) [ ]
Post town [ ]
County / Region [ ] Postcode [ ]
Country [ ]

Other change *(please specify)* [ ]

A serving director, secretary etc must sign the form below.

* Voluntary details.
† Directors only.
**Delete as appropriate.

Signed [ ] **Date** [ ]

(**director / secretary / administrator / administrative receiver / receiver manager / receiver)

Please give the name, address, telephone number and, if available, a DX number and Exchange of the person Companies House should contact if there is any query.

[ ]

Tel [ ]
DX number [ ] DX exchange [ ]

When you have completed and signed the form please send it to the Registrar of Companies at:
Companies House, Crown Way, Cardiff, CF14 3UZ   DX 33050 Cardiff
for companies registered in England and Wales   **or**
Companies House, 37 Castle Terrace, Edinburgh, EH1 2EB
for companies registered in Scotland   **DX 235 Edinburgh**

Companies House receipt date barcode

Form revised July 1998

JFL0011 / Rev 5.8   10/99

Form 11: 287 Notice of change in situation of registered office

JORDANS

287

Please complete in typescript, or in bold black capitals.
CHFP001

Change in situation or address of Registered Office

Company Number

Company Name in full

New situation of registered office

NOTE:

The change in the situation of the registered office does not take effect until the Registrar has registered this notice.

For 14 days beginning with the date that a change of registered office is registered, a person may validly serve any document on the company at its previous registered office.

PO Box numbers only are not acceptable.

Address

Post town

County / Region   **Postcode**

Signed   **Date**

† Please delete as appropriate.

† a director / secretary / administrator / administrative receiver / liquidator / receiver manager / receiver

Please give the name, address, telephone number and, if available, a DX number and Exchange of the person Companies House should contact if there is any query.

Tel

DX number   DX exchange

Companies House receipt date barcode

When you have completed and signed the form please send it to the Registrar of Companies at:
Companies House, Crown Way, Cardiff, CF14 3UZ   DX 33050 Cardiff
for companies registered in England and Wales
or
Companies House, 37 Castle Terrace, Edinburgh, EH1 2EB
for companies registered in Scotland   **DX 235 Edinburgh**

JFL0012 / Rev 5.4   10/99

Form 12: 88(2) Return of allotment of shares

Form 12: 88(2) Return of allotment of shares

JORDANS

*Please complete in typescript,
or in bold black capitals.*
CHFP001

88(2)

Return of Allotment of Shares

Company Number

Company name in full

Shares allotted (including bonus shares):

	From			To		
Date or period during which shares were allotted *(If shares were allotted on one date enter that date in the "from" box.)*	Day	Month	Year	Day	Month	Year

Class of shares
(ordinary or preference etc)

Number allotted

Nominal value of each share

Amount (if any) paid or due on each share *(including any share premium)*

List the names and addresses of the allottees and the number of shares allotted to each overleaf

If the allotted shares are fully or partly paid up otherwise than in cash please state:

% that each share is to be
treated as paid up

Consideration for which
the shares were allotted
*(This information must be supported by
the duly stamped contract or by the duly
stamped particulars on Form 88(3) if the
contract is not in writing)*

When you have completed and signed the form send it to the Registrar of Companies at:

Companies House receipt date barcode

Companies House, Crown Way, Cardiff CF14 3UZ   DX 33050 Cardiff
For companies registered in England and Wales

Companies House, 37 Castle Terrace, Edinburgh EH1 2EB   DX 235
For companies registered in Scotland   Edinburgh

10/99

Form 12: 88(2) Return of allotment of shares

Names and addresses of the allottees *(List joint share allotments consecutively)*

Shareholder details	Shares and share class allotted	
Name _____	Class of shares allotted	Number allotted
Address _____ _____	L_____ L____	
	L_____ L____	
UK Postcode L L L L L L L	L_____ L____	
Name _____	Class of shares allotted	Number allotted
Address _____ _____	L_____ L____	
	L_____ L____	
UK Postcode L L L L L L L	L_____ L____	
Name _____	Class of shares allotted	Number allotted
Address _____ _____	L_____ L____	
	L_____ L____	
UK Postcode L L L L L L L	L_____ L____	
Name _____	Class of shares allotted	Number allotted
Address _____ _____	L_____ L____	
	L_____ L____	
UK Postcode L L L L L L L	L_____ L____	
Name _____	Class of shares allotted	Number allotted
Address _____ _____	L_____ L____	
	L_____ L____	
UK Postcode L L L L L L L	L_____ L____	

Please enter the number of continuation sheet(s) (if any) attached to this form [   ]

Signed _____ **Date** _____

A director / secretary / administrator / administrative receiver / receiver manager / receiver   *Please delete as appropriate*

Please give the name, address, telephone number and, if available, a DX number and Exchange of the person Companies House should contact if there is any query.	
	Tel
DX number	DX exchange

10/99

Form 13: Jordans standard form for a Share Company

THE COMPANIES ACTS 1985 to 1989

PRIVATE COMPANY LIMITED BY SHARES

MEMORANDUM OF ASSOCIATION OF

*

1. The Company's name is '   '.

2. The Company's registered office is to be situated in England and Wales.

3. The Company's objects are:

3.1.1   To manage and administer the freehold or leasehold property or properties known as

(hereinafter called 'the Estate') and any other land, buildings and real property, either on its own account or as trustee, nominee or agent of any other company or person.

3.1.2   To acquire and deal with and take options over any property, real or personal, including the Estate, and any rights or privileges of any kind over or in respect of any property, and to improve, develop, sell, lease, accept, surrender or dispose of or otherwise deal with all or any part of such property and any and all rights of the Company therein or thereto.

3.1.3   To collect all rents, charges and other income and to pay any rates, taxes, charges, duties, levies, assessments or other outgoings of whatsoever nature charged, assessed, or imposed on or in respect of the Estate or any part thereof.

3.1.4   To provide services of every description in relation to the Estate and to maintain, repair, renew, redecorate, repaint, clean, construct, alter and add to the Estate and to arrange for the supply to it of services and amenities and the maintenance of the same and the cultivation, maintenance, landscaping and planting of any land, gardens and grounds comprised in the Estate and to enter into contracts with builders, tenants, contractors and others and to employ appropriate staff and managing or other agents whatsoever in relation thereto.

3.1.5   To insure the Estate or any other property of the Company or in which it has an interest against damage or destruction and such other risks as may be considered necessary, appropriate or desirable and to insure the Company against public liability and any other risks which it may consider prudent or desirable to insure against.

3.1.6   To establish and maintain capital reserves, management funds and any form of sinking fund in order to pay or contribute towards all fees, costs, and other expenses incurred in the implementation of the Company's objects and to require the members of the Company to contribute towards such reserves or funds at such times, in such amounts and in such manner as the Company may think fit and to invest and deal in and with such moneys not immediately required in such manner as may from time to time be determined.

3.2   To carry on any other trade or business whatever which can in the opinion of the board of directors be advantageously carried on in connection with or ancillary to any of the businesses of the Company.

3.3   To improve, manage, construct, repair, develop, exchange, let on lease or otherwise, mortgage, charge, sell, dispose of, turn to account, grant licences, options, rights and privileges in respect of, or otherwise deal with all or any part of the property and rights of the Company.

3.4   To invest and deal with the moneys of the Company not immediately required in such manner as may from time to time be determined and to hold or otherwise deal with any investments made.

3.5   To lend and advance money or give credit on any terms and with our without security to any person, firm or company, to enter into guarantees, contracts of indemnity and suretyships of all kinds, to receive money on deposit or loan upon any terms, and to secure or guarantee in any manner and upon any terms the payment of any sum of money or the performance of any obligation by any person, firm or company.

3.6   To borrow and raise money in any manner and to secure the repayment of any money borrowed, raised or owing by mortgage, charge, standard security, lien or other security upon the whole or any part of the Company's property or assets (whether present or future), including its uncalled capital, and also by a similar mortgage, charge, standard security, lien or security to secure and guarantee the performance by the Company of any obligation or liability it may undertake or which may become binding on it.

3.7   To draw, make, accept, endorse, discount, negotiate, execute and issue cheques, bills of exchange, promissory notes, bills of lading, warrants, debentures, and other negotiable or transferable instruments.

3.8   To enter into any arrangements with any government or authority (supreme, municipal, local, or otherwise) that may seem conducive to the attainment of the Company's objects or any of them, and to obtain from any such government or authority any charters, decrees, rights, privileges or concessions which the Company may think desirable and to carry out, exercise, and comply with any such charters, decrees, rights, privileges, and concessions.

3.9   To pay all or any expenses incurred in connection with the promotion, formation and incorporation of the Company, or to contract with any person, firm or company to pay the same, and to pay commissions to brokers and others for underwriting, placing, selling, or guaranteeing the subscription of any shares or other securities of the Company.

3.10   To give or award pensions, annuities, gratuities, and superannuation or other allowances or benefits or charitable aid and generally to provide advantages, facilities and services for any persons who are or have been directors of, or who are or have been employed by, or who are serving or have served the Company and to the wives, widows, children and other relatives and dependants of such persons; to make payments towards insurance including insurance for any director, officer or auditor against any liability in respect of any negligence, default, breach of duty or breach of trust (so far as permitted by law); and to set up, establish, support and maintain superannuation and other funds or schemes (whether contributory or non-contributory) for the benefit of any of such persons and of their wives, widows, children and other relatives and dependants.

3.11   Subject to and in accordance with the provisions of the Act (if and so far as such provisions shall be applicable) to give, directly or indirectly, financial assistance for the acquisition of shares or other securities of the Company or of any other company or for the reduction or discharge of any liability incurred in respect of such acquisition.

3.12   To distribute among the members of the Company in kind any property of the Company of whatever nature.

3.13   To do all or any of the things or matters aforesaid in any part of the world and either as principals, agents, contractors or otherwise, and by or through agents, brokers, sub-contractors or otherwise and either alone or in conjunction with others.

3.14   To do all such other things as may be deemed incidental or conducive to the attainment of the Company's objects or any of them.

3.15   AND so that:

3.15.1   None of the objects set forth in any sub-clause of this clause shall be restrictively construed but the widest interpretation shall be given to each such object, and none of such objects shall, except where the context expressly so requires, be in any way limited or restricted by reference to or inference from any other object or objects set forth in such sub-clause, or by reference to or inference from the terms of any other sub-clause of this clause, or by reference to or inference from the name of the Company.

3.15.2   None of the sub-clauses of this clause and none of the objects therein specified shall be deemed subsidiary or ancillary to any of the objects specified in any other such sub-clause, and the Company shall have as full a power to exercise each and every one of the objects specified in each sub-clause of this clause as though each such sub-clause contained the objects of a separate Company.

3.15.3   The word 'company' in this clause, except where used in reference to the Company, shall be deemed to include any partnership or other body of persons, whether incorporated or unincorporated and whether domiciled in the United Kingdom or elsewhere.

3.15.4   In this clause the expression 'the Act' means the Companies Act 1985, but so that any reference in this clause to any provision of the Act shall be deemed to include a reference to any statutory modification or re-enactment of that provision for the time being in force.

4.   The liability of the members is limited.

5.   The Company's share capital is £   divided into   shares of £   each.

Form 13: Jordans standard form for a Share Company

THE COMPANIES ACTS 1985 to 1989

PRIVATE COMPANY LIMITED BY SHARES

ARTICLES OF ASSOCIATION OF

*

1. PRELIMINARY

1.1   The regulations contained in Table A in the Schedule to the Companies (Tables A to F) Regulations 1985 (SI 1985 No. 805) as amended by the Companies (Tables A to F) (Amendment) Regulations 1985 (SI 1985 No. 1052) (such Table being hereinafter called 'Table A') shall apply to the Company save in so far as they are excluded or varied hereby and such regulations (save as so excluded or varied) and the Articles hereinafter contained shall be the Articles of Association of the Company.

1.2   In these Articles:

'the Act'	means the Companies Act 1985, but so that any reference in these Articles to any provision of the Act shall be deemed to include a reference to any statutory modification or re-enactment of that provision for the time being in force.
'the Estate'	shall have the meaning assigned to it in the Memorandum of Association but shall also include any other land, building or premises for the time being also owned and/or managed or administered by the Company;
'dwelling'	means any residential unit comprised in the Estate;
'dwellingholder'	means the person or persons to whom a lease or tenancy of a dwelling has been granted or assigned or who holds the freehold of a dwelling and so that whenever two or more persons are for the time being dwellingholders of a dwelling they shall for all purposes of these Articles be deemed to constitute one dwellingholder.

Form 13: Jordans standard form for a Share Company

2. ALLOTMENT AND TRANSFER OF SHARES

2.1.1 The subscribers to the Memorandum of Association of the Company shall be duly registered as members of the Company in respect of the shares for which they have subscribed. A subscriber may transfer any shares subscribed by him to a person nominated by him in writing to succeed him as a member and any such person (other than a dwellingholder) so nominated shall have the same power to transfer the share as if he had himself been a subscriber. Personal representatives of a deceased subscriber or of any successor so nominated by him shall have the same rights of transfer.

2.1.2 Save as aforesaid, no share shall be allotted or transferred to any person who is not a dwellingholder. A dwellingholder shall not be entitled to dispose of his shareholding in the Company while holding, whether alone or jointly with others, a legal estate in any dwelling.

2.1.3 In accordance with section 91(1) of the Act sections 89(1) and 90(1) to (6) (inclusive) of the Act shall not apply to the Company.

2.1.4 Subject as provided in Article 2.1.2 above the directors are generally and unconditionally authorised for the purposes of section 80 of the Act, to exercise any power of the Company to allot and grant rights to subscribe for or convert securities into shares of the Company up to the amount of the authorised share capital with which the Company up to the amount of the authorised share capital with which the Company is incorporated at any time or times during the period of five years from the date of incorporation and the directors may, after that period, allot any shares or grant any such rights under this authority in pursuance of an offer or agreement so to do made by the Company within that period. The authority hereby given may at any time (subject to the said section 80) be renewed, revoked or varied by ordinary resolution.

2.2.1 If any member of the Company who is a dwellingholder parts with all interest in the dwelling or dwellings held by him, or if his interest therein for any reason ceases and determines, he or, in the event of his death, his legal personal representative or representatives, or in the event of his bankruptcy, his trustee in bankruptcy shall transfer his shareholding in the Company to the person or persons who become the dwellingholder of the dwelling or dwellings.

2.2.2   Each subscriber to the Memorandum of Association and any person becoming a member as a result of a nomination under Article 2.1.1 above shall, if not himself a dwellingholder, offer his shareholding in the Company to the Company as soon as dwellingholders for all the dwellings have become members. The Company shall:

(a) subject to the provisions of the Act, purchase such shareholding in which case the member concerned shall execute all such documents (including any contract required under section 164 of the Act) and do all such acts and things as may be necessary in order to enable the Company to comply with the Act and effect such purchase; or

(b) direct the member concerned to transfer his shareholding to some other dwellingholder or dwellingholders in which case the member concerned shall execute a share transfer in respect of his shareholding as appropriate and deliver the same to the Company PROVIDED that the sanction of a special resolution shall be required for any such transfer where the proposed transferee or transferees already hold one share of the Company in respect of each of their dwellings.

2.2.3   The price to be paid on the transfer of every share under this Article shall, unless (in the case of a transfer made pursuant to Article 2.2.1 above) the transferor and transferee otherwise agree, be its nominal value.

2.2.4   If the holder of a share (or his legal personal representative or representatives or trustee in bankruptcy) refuses or neglects to transfer it or offer it for purchase in accordance with this Article, one of the directors, duly nominated for that purpose by a resolution of the board, shall be the attorney of such holder, with full power on his behalf and in his name to execute, complete and deliver a transfer of his share to the person or persons to whom the same ought to be transferred hereunder or (as the case may be) any documentation as is referred to in Article 2.2.2 above; and the Company may give a good discharge for the purchase money and (in the case of a transfer) enter the name of the transferee of the said share in the register of members as the holder thereof.

2.3   If a member shall die or be adjudged bankrupt, his legal personal representative or representatives or the trustee in his bankruptcy shall be entitled to be registered as a member of the

Company, provided he or they shall for the time being be a dwellingholder.

2.4.1   The directors shall refuse to register any transfer of shares made in contravention of all the foregoing provisions of these Articles, but otherwise shall have no power to refuse to register a transfer.

2.4.2   Regulation 24 in Table A shall not apply to the Company.

3.   SHARES

3.1   The lien conferred by regulation 8 in Table A shall attach also to fully paid-up shares, and the Company shall also have a first and paramount lien on all shares, whether fully paid or not, standing registered in the name of any person indebted or under liability to the Company, whether he shall be the sole registered holder thereof or shall be one of two or more joint holders, for all moneys presently payable by him or his estate to the Company. Regulation 8 in Table A shall be modified accordingly.

3.2   The liability of any member in default in respect of a call shall be increased by the addition at the end of the first sentence of regulation 18 in Table A of the words 'and all expenses that may have been incurred by the Company by reason of such non-payment'.

4.   GENERAL MEETINGS AND RESOLUTIONS

4.1   Every notice convening a general meeting shall comply with the provisions of section 372(3) of the Act as to giving information to members in regard to their right to appoint proxies; and notices of and other communications relating to any general meeting which any member is entitled to receive shall be sent to the directors and to the auditors for the time being of the Company.

4.2.1   If a quorum is not present within half an hour from the time appointed for a general meeting the general meeting shall stand adjourned to the same day in the next week at the same time and place or to such other day and at such other time and place as the directors may determine; and if at the adjourned general meeting a quorum is not present within half an hour from the time appointed therefor such adjourned general meeting shall be dissolved.

4.2.2   Regulation 41 in Table A shall not apply to the Company.

4.3   Resolutions under section 303 of the Act for the removal of a director before the expiration of his period of office and under section 391 of the Act for the removal of an auditor before the expiration of his period of office shall only be considered by the Company in general meeting.

4.4   A member present at a meeting by proxy shall be entitled to speak at the meeting.

4.5   Unless resolved by ordinary resolution that regulation 62 in Table A shall apply without modification, the instrument appointing a proxy and any authority under which it is executed or a copy of such authority certified notarially or in some other way approved by the directors may be deposited at the place specified in regulation 62 in Table A up to the commencement of the meeting or (in any case where a poll is taken otherwise than at the meeting) of the taking of the poll or may be handed to the chairman of the meeting prior to the commencement of the business of the meeting.

5.   VOTES OF MEMBERS

5.1   Every member present in person or by proxy or, being a corporation, present by a duly authorised representative at a general meeting shall have one vote PROVIDED that where no dwellingholder exists in respect of any dwelling, those members who are subscribers to the Memorandum of Association or who became members as a result of having been nominated under Article 2.1.1 above or, if there is only such member or person nominated under Article 2.1.1 above, that member, shall, either jointly if there is more than one such member, or alone, if there is only one such member, have three votes in respect of every dwelling in addition to their own vote or votes as members whether voting is by a show of hands or on a poll.

5.2   Regulation 54 in Table A shall not apply to the Company.

6.   APPOINTMENT OF DIRECTORS

6.1.1   Regulation 64 in Table A shall not apply to the Company.

6.1.2   The maximum number and minimum number respectively of the directors may be determined from time to time by ordinary resolution. Subject to and in default of any such determination there shall be no maximum number of directors and the minimum number of directors shall be two.

6.2   The directors shall not be required to retire by rotation and regulations 73 to 80 (inclusive) in Table A shall not apply to the Company.

6.3   No person shall be appointed a director at any general meeting unless either:

(a) he is recommended by the directors; or

(b) not less than 14 nor more than 35 clear days before the date appointed for the general meeting, notice signed by a member qualified to vote at the general meeting has been given to the Company of the intention to propose that person for appointment, together with notice signed by that person of his willingness to be appointed.

6.4.1   Subject to Article 6.3 above, the Company may by ordinary resolution appoint any person who is willing to act to be a director, either to fill a vacancy or as an additional director.

6.4.2   The directors may appoint a person who is willing to act to be a director, either to fill a vacancy or as an additional director, provided that the appointment does not cause the number of directors to exceed any number determined in accordance with Article 6.1.2 above as the maximum number of directors and for the time being in force.

7.   BORROWING POWERS

7.1   The directors may exercise all the powers of the Company to borrow money without limit as to amount and upon such terms and in such manner as they think fit, and subject (in the case of any security convertible into shares) to section 80 of the Act to grant any mortgage, charge or standard security over its undertaking, property and uncalled capital, or any part thereof, and to issue debentures, debenture stock, and other securities whether outright or as security for any debt, liability or obligation of the Company or of any third party.

8.   ALTERNATE DIRECTORS

8.1   Unless otherwise determined by the Company in general meeting by ordinary resolution an alternate director shall not be entitled as such to receive any remuneration from the Company, save that he may be paid by the Company such part (if any) of the remuneration otherwise payable to his appointor as such appointor may by notice in writing to the Company from time to time direct, and the first sentence of regulation 66 in Table A shall be modified accordingly.

8.2   A director, or any such other person as is mentioned in regulation 65 in Table A, may act as an alternate director to represent more than one director, and an alternate director shall be entitled at any meeting of the directors or of any committee of the directors to one vote for every director whom he represents in addition to his own vote (if any) as a director, but he shall count as only one for the purpose of determining whether a quorum is present.

9.   GRATUITIES AND PENSIONS

9.1.1   The directors may exercise the powers of the Company conferred by its Memorandum of Association in relation to the payment of pensions, gratuities and other benefits and shall be entitled to retain any benefits received by them or any of them by reason of the exercise of any such powers.

9.1.2   Regulation 87 in Table A shall not apply to the Company.

10.   PROCEEDINGS OF DIRECTORS

10.1.1   A director may vote, at any meeting of the directors or of any committee of the directors, on any resolution, notwithstanding that it in any way concerns or relates to a matter in which he has, directly or indirectly, any kind of interest whatsoever, and if he shall vote on any such resolution his vote shall be counted; and in relation to any such resolution as aforesaid he shall (whether or not he shall vote on the same) be taken into account in calculating the quorum present at the meeting.

10.1.2   Each director shall comply with his obligations to disclose his interest in contracts under section 317 of the Act.

10.1.3   Regulations 94 to 97 (inclusive) in Table A shall not apply to the Company.

11.   THE SEAL

11.1   If the Company has a seal it shall only be used with the authority of the directors or of a committee of directors. The directors may determine who shall sign any instrument to which the seal is affixed and unless otherwise so determined it shall be signed by a director and by the secretary or second director. The obligation under regulation 6 of Table A relating to the sealing of share certificates shall apply only if the Company has a seal. Regulation 101 in Table A shall not apply to the Company.

12. NOTICES

12.1   Without prejudice to regulations 112 to 116 inclusive in Table A, the Company may give notice to a member by electronic means provided that:

12.1.1   the member has given his consent in writing to receiving notice communicated by electronic means and in such consent has set out an address to which the notice shall be sent by electronic means; and

12.1.2   the electronic means used by the Company enables the member concerned to read the text of the notice.

12.2   A notice given to a member personally or in a form permitted by Article 12.1 above shall be deemed to be given on the earlier of the day on which it is delivered personally and the day on which it was despatched by electronic means, as the case may be.

12.3   Regulation 115 in Table A shall not apply to a notice delivered personally or in a form permitted by Article 12.1 above.

12.4   In this article 'electronic' means actuated by electric, magnetic, electro-magnetic, electro-chemical or electro-mechanical energy and 'by electronic means' means by any manner only capable of being so actuated.

13. INDEMNITY

13.1   Every director or other officer or auditor of the Company shall be indemnified out of the assets of the Company against all losses or liabilities which he may sustain or incur in or about the execution of the duties of his office or otherwise in relation thereto, incuding any liability incurred by him in defending any proceedings, whether civil or criminal, or in connection with any application under section 144 or section 727 of the Act in which relief is granted to him by the Court, and no director or other officer shall be liable for any loss, damage or misfortune which may happen to or be incurred by the Company in the execution of the duties of his office or in relation thereto. But this Article shall only have effect in so far as its provisions are not avoided by section 310 of the Act.

13.2   The directors shall have power to purchase and maintain for any director, officer or auditor of the Company insurance against any such liability as is referred to in section 310(1) of the Act.

13.3   Regulation 118 in Table A shall not apply to the Company.

14.   RULES OR BYELAWS

14.1   The directors may from time to time make such rules or bye-laws as they may deem necessary or expedient or convenient for the proper conduct and management of the Company and for the purposes of prescribing the classes of and conditions of membership, and in particular but without prejudice to the generality of the foregoing, they shall by such rules or bye-laws regulate:

(a) the admission and classification of members of the Company, and the rights and privileges of such members, and the conditions of membership and the terms on which members may resign or have their membership terminated and the entrance fees, subscriptions and other fees, charges, contributions or payments to be made by members;

(b) the conduct of members of the Company in relation to one another, and to the Company and to the Company's servants or agents;

(c) the setting aside of the whole or any part or parts of the Estate at any particular time or times or for a particular purpose or purposes;

(d) the procedure at general meetings and meetings of the directors and committees of the directors of the Company insofar as such procedure is not regulated by these Articles;

(e) and, generally, all such matters as are commonly the subject matter of company rules or rules or regulations appropriate to property of a similar nature and type as the Estate.

14.2   The Company in general meeting shall have power to alter or repeal the rules or bye-laws and to make additions thereto and the directors shall adopt such means as they deem sufficient to bring to the notice of members of the Company all such rules or bye-laws, which so long as they shall be in force, shall be binding on all members of the Company. Provided, nevertheless, that no rule or bye-law shall be inconsistent with, or shall affect or repeal anything contained in, the Memorandum or Articles of Association of the Company.

Form 14: Jordans standard form for a Guarantee Company

THE COMPANIES ACTS 1985 to 1989

COMPANY LIMITED BY GUARANTEE AND NOT HAVING A SHARE CAPITAL

MEMORANDUM OF ASSOCIATION OF

*

1. The Company's name is '   '.

2. The Company's registered office is to be situated in England and Wales.

3. The Company's objects are:

3.1.1   To manage and administer the freehold or leasehold property or properties known as

(hereinafter called 'the Estate') and any other land, buildings and real property, either on its own account or as trustee, nominee or agent of any other company or person.

3.1.2   To acquire and deal with and take options over any property, real or personal, including the Estate, and any rights or privileges of any kind over or in respect of any property, and to improve, develop, sell, lease, accept, surrender or dispose of or otherwise deal with all or any part of such property and any and all rights of the Company therein or thereto.

3.1.3   To collect all rents, charges and other income and to pay any rates, taxes, charges, duties, levies, assessments or other outgoings of whatsoever nature charged, assessed, or imposed on or in respect of the Estate or any part thereof.

3.1.4   To provide services of every description in relation to the Estate and to maintain, repair, renew, redecorate, repaint, clean, construct, alter and add to the Estate and to arrange for the supply to it of services and amenities and the maintenance of the same and the cultivation, maintenance, landscaping and planting of any land, gardens and grounds comprised in the Estate and to enter into contracts with builders, tenants, contractors and others and to employ appropriate staff and managing or other agents whatsoever in relation thereto.

3.1.5   To insure the Estate or any other property of the Company or in which it has an interest against damage or destruction and such other risks as may be considered necessary, appropriate or desirable and to insure the Company against public liability and any other risks which it may consider prudent or desirable to insure against.

3.1.6   To establish and maintain capital reserves, management funds and any form of sinking fund in order to pay or contribute towards all fees, costs, and other expenses incurred in the implementation of the Company's objects and to require the members of the Company to contribute towards such reserves or funds at such times, in such amounts and in such manner as the Company may think fit and to invest and deal in and with such moneys not immediately required in such manner as may from time to time be determined.

3.2   To carry on any other trade or business whatever which can in the opinion of the board of directors be advantageously carried on in connection with or ancillary to any of the businesses of the Company.

3.3   To improve, manage, construct, repair, develop, exchange, let on lease or otherwise, mortgage, charge, sell, dispose of, turn to account, grant licences, options, rights and privileges in respect of, or otherwise deal with all or any part of the property and rights of the Company.

3.4   To invest and deal with the moneys of the Company not immediately required in such manner as may from time to time be determined and to hold or otherwise deal with any investments made.

3.5   To lend and advance money or give credit on any terms and with or without security to any person, firm or company, to enter into guarantees, contracts of indemnity and suretyships of all kinds, to receive money on deposit or loan upon any terms, and to secure or guarantee in any manner and upon any terms the payment of any sum of money or the performance of any obligation by any person, firm or company.

3.6   To borrow and raise money in any manner and to secure the repayment of any money borrowed, raised or owing by mortgage, charge, standard security, lien or other security upon the whole or any part of the Company's property or assets (whether present or future), including its uncalled capital, and also by a similar mortgage, charge, standard security, lien or security to secure and guarantee the performance by the Company of any obligation or liability it may undertake or which may become binding on it.

3.7   To draw, make, accept, endorse, discount, negotiate, execute and issue cheques, bills of exchange, promissory notes, bills of lading, warrants, debentures, and other negotiable or transferable instruments.

3.8   To enter into any arrangements with any government or authority (supreme, municipal, local, or otherwise) that may seem conducive to the attainment of the Company's objects or any of them, and to obtain from any such government or authority any charters, decrees, rights, privileges or concessions which the Company may think desirable and to carry out, exercise, and comply with any such charters, decrees, rights, privileges, and concessions.

3.9   To pay all or any expenses incurred in connection with the promotion, formation and incorporation of the Company, or to contract with any person, firm or company to pay the same.

3.10   To give or award pensions, annuities, gratuities, and superannuation or other allowances or benefits or charitable aid and generally to provide advantages, facilities and services for any persons who are or have been Directors of, or who are or have been employed by, or who are serving or have served the Company and to the wives, widows, children and other relatives and dependants of such persons; to make payments towards insurance including insurance for any Director, officer or Auditor against any liability as is referred to in Section 310(1) of the Act; and to set up, establish, support and maintain superannuation and other funds or schemes (whether contributory or non-contributory) for the benefit of any of such persons and of their wives, widows, children and other relatives and dependants.

3.11   To distribute among the members of the Company in kind any property of the Company of whatever nature.

3.12   To do all or any of the things or matters aforesaid in any part of the world and either as principals, agents, contractors or otherwise, and by or through agents, brokers, sub-contractors or otherwise and either alone or in conjunction with others.

3.13   To do all such other things as may be deemed incidental or conducive to the attainment of the Company's objects or any of them.

3.14   AND so that:

3.14.1   None of the objects set forth in any sub-clause of this clause shall be restrictively construed but the widest interpretation shall be given to each such object, and none of such objects shall, except where the context expressly so requires, be in any way limited or restricted by reference to or inference from any other object or objects set forth in such sub-clause, or by reference to or inference from the terms of any other sub-clause of this clause, or by reference to or inference from the name of the Company.

3.14.2   None of the sub-clauses of this clause and none of the objects therein specified shall be deemed subsidiary or ancillary to any of the objects specified in any other such sub-clause, and the Company shall have as full a power to exercise each and every one of the objects specified in each sub-clause of this clause as though each such sub-clause contained the objects of a separate Company.

3.14.3   The word 'company' in this clause, except where used in reference to the Company, shall be deemed to include any partnership or other body of persons, whether incorporated or unincorporated and whether domiciled in the United Kingdom or elsewhere.

3.14.4   In this clause the expression 'the Act' means the Companies Act 1985, but so that any reference in this clause to any provision of the Act shall be deemed to include a reference to any statutory modification or re-enactment of that provision for the time being in force.

4.   The liability of the members is limited.

5.   Every member of the Company undertakes to contribute such amount as may be required (not exceeding £1) to the Company's assets if it should be wound up while he is a member or within one year after he ceases to be a member, for payment of the Company's debts and liabilities contracted before he ceases to be a member, and of the costs, charges and expenses of winding up, and for the adjustment of the rights of the contributions among themselves.

Form 14: Jordans standard form for a Guarantee Company

THE COMPANIES ACTS 1985 to 1989

COMPANY LIMITED BY GUARANTEE AND NOT HAVING A SHARE CAPITAL

ARTICLES OF ASSOCIATION OF

*

1. PRELIMINARY

1.1   The regulations contained in Table A in the Schedule to the Companies (Tables A to F) Regulations 1985 (SI 1985 No. 805) as amended by the Companies (Tables A to F) (Amendment) Regulations 1985 (SI 1985 No. 1052) (such Table being hereinafter called 'Table A') shall apply to the Company save in so far as they are excluded or varied hereby and such regulations (save as so excluded or varied) and the Articles hereinafter contained shall be the Articles of Association of the Company.

1.2   Regulations 2 to 35 (inclusive), 57, 59, 102 to 108 (inclusive), 110, 114, 116 and 117 in Table A shall not apply to the Company.

2. INTERPRETATION

2.1   In these Articles:

'the Act'   means the Companies Act 1985, but so that any reference in these Articles to any provision of the Act shall be deemed to include a reference to any statutory modification or re-enactment of that provision for the time being in force.

'the Estate'   shall have the meaning assigned to it in the Memorandum of Association but shall also include any other land, building or premises for the time being also owned and/or managed or administered by the Company;

'dwelling'   means any residential unit comprised in the Estate;

'dwellingholder'   means the person or persons to whom a lease or tenancy of a dwelling has been granted or assigned or who holds the freehold of a dwelling and so that whenever two or more persons are for the time being dwellingholders of a dwelling they shall for all purposes of these Articles be deemed to constitute one dwellingholder.

2.2 Regulation 1 in Table A shall be read and construed as if the definition of 'the holder' were omitted therefrom.

3. MEMBERS

3.1 The subscribers to the Memorandum of Association shall be members of the Company. A subscriber may nominate any person to succeed him as a member of the Company and any person so nominated (other than a dwellingholder) shall have the same power to nominate a person to succeed him as if he had been a subscriber. Save as aforesaid, no person shall be admitted as a member of the Company other than a dwellingholder. The Company must accept as a member every person who is or who shall have become entitled to be admitted as a member and shall have complied with either of the signature provisions set out in Article 3.3 below.

3.2 Each subscriber to the Memorandum of Association and any person nominated to be a member under Article 3.1 above shall, if not himself a dwellingholder, cease to be a member as soon as dwellingholders for all the dwellings have become members.

3.3 The provisions of section 352 of the Act shall be observed by the Company and every member of the Company other than the subscribers to the Memorandum of Association shall either sign a written consent to become a member or sign the register of members on becoming a member. If two or more persons are together a dwellingholder each shall so comply, they shall together constitute one member and the person whose name first appears in the register of members shall exercise the voting powers vested in such member.

3.4 A dwellingholder shall cease to be a member on the registration as a member of the successor to his dwelling and shall not resign as a member while holding, whether alone or jointly with others, a legal estate in any dwelling.

3.5 If a member shall die or be adjuged bankrupt his legal personal representative or representatives or the trustee in his bankruptcy shall be entitled to be registered as a member provided that he or they shall for the time being be a dwellingholder.

Form 14: Jordans standard form for a Guarantee Company

4. GENERAL MEETINGS AND RESOLUTIONS

4.1   An annual general meeting and an extraordinary general meeting called for the passing of a special resolution or a resolution appointing a person as a director shall be called by at least 21 clear days' notice. All other extraordinary general meetings shall be called by at least 14 clear days' notice but a general meeting may be called by shorter notice if it is so agreed:

   (a) in the case of an annual general meeting, by all the members entitled to attend and vote thereat; and

   (b) in the case of any other general meeting by a majority in number of the Members having a right to attend and vote being a majority together holding (subject to the provisions of any elective resolution of the Company for the time being in force) not less than 95% of the total voting rights at the meeting of all members.

4.1.2   The notice shall specify the time and place of the meeting and, in the case of an annual general meeting, shall specify the meeting as such.

4.1.3   The notice shall be given to all the members and to the directors and auditors and to every legal personal representative or trustee in bankruptcy of a member where the member, but for his death or bankruptcy, would be entitled to receive notice of the meeting.

4.1.4   Regulation 38 in Table A shall not apply to the Company.

4.2.1   If a quorum is not present within half an hour from the time appointed for a general meeting the general meeting shall stand adjourned to the same day in the next week at the same time and place or to such other day and at such other time and place as the directors may determine; and if at the adjourned general meeting a quorum is not present within half an hour from the time appointed therefor such adjourned general meeting shall be dissolved.

4.2.2   Regulation 41 in Table A shall not apply to the Company.

4.3   Resolutions under section 303 of the Act for the removal of a director before the expiration of his period of office and under section 391 of the Act for the removal of an auditor before the expiration of his period of office shall only be considered by the Company in general meeting.

4.4.1   Regulation 44 in Table A shall be read and construed as if the words 'and at any separate meeting of the holders of any class of shares in the Company' were omitted therefrom.

4.4.2   Regulation 46 in Table A shall be read and construed as if paragraph (d) was omitted therefrom.

4.5.1   Any member of the Company entitled to attend and vote at a general meeting shall be entitled to appoint another person (whether a member or not) as his proxy to attend and vote instead of him and any proxy so appointed shall have the same right as the member to speak at the meeting.

4.5.2   Every member present in person or by proxy or, being a corporation, present by a duly authorised representative at a general meeting shall have one vote PROVIDED that where no dwellingholder exists in respect of any dwelling, those members who are subscribers to the Memorandum of Association or who became members as a result of having been nominated by a subscriber to the Memorandum of Association under Article 3.1 above or, if there is only one such member or person nominated under Article 3.1 above, that member, shall, either jointly if there is more than one such member, or alone, if there is only one such member, have three votes in respect of every dwelling in addition to their own vote or votes as members whether voting is by a show of hands or on a poll.

4.5.3   Regulations 54 and 55 in Table A shall not apply to the Company.

4.6   Unless resolved by ordinary resolution that regulation 62 in Table A shall apply without modification, the instrument appointing a proxy and any authority under which it is executed or a copy of such authority certified notarially or in some other way approved by the directors may be deposited at the place specified in regulation 62 in Table A up to the commencement of the meeting or (in any case where a poll is taken otherwise than at the meeting) of the taking of the poll or may be handed to the chairman of the meeting prior to the commencement of the business of the meeting.

5.   APPOINTMENT OF DIRECTORS

5.1.1   Regulation 64 in Table A shall not apply to the Company.

5.1.2   The maximum number and minimum number respectively

of the directors may be determined from time to time by ordinary resolution. Subject to and in default of any such determination there shall be no maximum number of directors and the minimum number of directors shall be two.

5.2   The directors shall not be required to retire by rotation and regulations 73 to 80 (inclusive) in Table A shall not apply to the Company.

5.3   Regulation 83 in Table A shall be read and construed as if the words 'of any class of shares or' were omitted therefrom.

5.4   No person shall be appointed a director at any general meeting unless either:

(a) he is recommended by the directors; or

(b) not less than 14 nor more than 35 clear days before the date appointed for the general meeting, notice signed by a member qualified to vote at the general meeting has been given to the Company of the intention to propose that person for appointment, together with notice signed by that person of his willingness to be appointed.

5.5.1   Subject to Article 5.4 above, the Company may by ordinary resolution appoint any person who is willing to act to be a director, either to fill a vacancy or as an additional director.

5.5.2   The directors may appoint a person who is willing to act to be a director, either to fill a vacancy or as an additional director, provided that the appointment does not cause the number of directors to exceed any number determined in accordance with Article 5.1.2 above as the maximum number of directors and for the time being in force.

6.   BORROWING POWERS

6.1   The directors may exercise all the powers of the Company to borrow money without limit as to amount and upon such terms and in such manner as they think fit, and to grant any mortgage, charge or standard security over its undertaking and property, or any part thereof, and to issue debentures, whether outright or as security for any debt, liability or obligation of the Company or of any third party.

7. ALTERNATE DIRECTORS

7.1 Unless otherwise determined by the Company in general meeting by ordinary resolution an alternate director shall not be entitled as such to receive any remuneration from the Company, save that he may be paid by the Company such part (if any) of the remuneration otherwise payable to his appointor as such appointor may by notice in writing to the Company from time to time direct, and the first sentence of regulation 66 in Table A shall be modified accordingly.

7.2 A director, or any such other person as is mentioned in regulation 65 in Table A, may act as an alternate director to represent more than one director, and an alternate director shall be entitled at any meeting of the directors or of any committee of the directors to one vote for every director whom he represents in addition to his own vote (if any) as a director, but he shall count as only one for the purpose of determining whether a quorum is present.

8. GRATUITIES AND PENSIONS

8.1.1 The directors may exercise the powers of the Company conferred by its Memorandum of Association in relation to the payment of pensions, gratuities and other benefits and shall be entitled to retain any benefits received by them or any of them by reason of the exercise of any such powers.

8.1.2 Regulation 87 in Table A shall not apply to the Company.

9. PROCEEDINGS OF DIRECTORS

9.1.1 A director may vote, at any meeting of the directors or of any committee of the directors, on any resolution, notwithstanding that it in any way concerns or relates to a matter in which he has, directly or indirectly, any kind of interest whatsoever, and if he shall vote on any such resolution his vote shall be counted; and in relation to any such resolution as aforesaid he shall (whether or not he shall vote on the same) be taken into account in calculating the quorum present at the meeting.

9.1.2 Each director shall comply with his obligations to disclose his interest in contracts under section 317 of the Act.

9.1.3 Regulations 94 to 97 (inclusive) in Table A shall not apply to the Company.

10. MINUTES

10.1   Regulation 100 in Table A shall be read and construed as if the words 'of the holders of any class of shares in the Company' were omitted therefrom.

11. THE SEAL

11.1   If the Company has a seal it shall only be used with the authority of the directors or of a committee of directors. The directors may determine who shall sign any instrument to which the seal is affixed and unless otherwise so determined it shall be signed by a director and by the secretary or second director. Regulation 101 in Table A shall not apply to the Company.

12. NOTICES

12.1   Without prejudice to regulations 112 to 116 inclusive in Table A, the Company may give notice to a member by electronic means provided that:

12.1.1   the member has given his consent in writing to receiving notice communicated by electronic means and in such consent has set out an address to which the notice shall be sent by electronic means; and

12.1.2   the electronic means used by the Company enables the member concerned to read the text of the notice.

12.2   A notice given to a member personally or in a form permitted by Article 12.1 above shall be deemed to be given on the earlier of the day on which it is delivered personally and the day on which it was despatched by electronic means, as the case may be.

12.3   Regulation 115 in Table A shall not apply to a notice delivered personally or in a form permitted by Article 12.1 above.

12.4   In this article 'electronic' means actuated by electric, magnetic, electro-magnetic, electro-chemical or electro-mechanical energy and 'by electronic means' means by any manner only capable of being so actuated.

12.5   Regulation 112 in Table A shall be read and construed as if the second sentence was omitted therefrom.

12.6   Regulation 113 in Table A shall be read and construed as if the words 'or of the holders of any class of shares in the Company' were omitted therefrom.

13.   INDEMNITY

13.1   Every director or other officer or auditor of the Company shall be indemnified out of the assets of the Company against all losses or liabilities which he may sustain or incur in or about the execution of the duties of his office or otherwise in relation thereto, incuding any liability incurred by him in defending any proceedings, whether civil or criminal, or in connection with any application under section 727 of the Act in which relief is granted to him by the Court, and no director or other officer shall be liable for any loss, damage or misfortune which may happen to or be incurred by the Company in the execution of the duties of his office or in relation thereto. But this Article shall only have effect in so far as its provisions are not avoided by section 310 of the Act.

13.2   The directors shall have power to purchase and maintain for any director, officer or auditor of the Company insurance against any such liability as is referred to in section 310(1) of the Act.

13.3   Regulation 118 in Table A shall not apply to the Company.

14.   RULES OR BYELAWS

14.1   The directors may from time to time make such rules or bye-laws as they may deem necessary or expedient or convenient for the proper conduct and management of the Company and for the purposes of prescribing the classes of and conditions of membership, and in particular but without prejudice to the generality of the foregoing, they shall by such rules or bye-laws regulate:

(a) the admission and classification of members of the Company, and the rights and privileges of such members, and the conditions of membership and the terms on which members may resign or have their membership terminated and the entrance fees, subscriptions and other fees, charges, contributions or payments to be made by members.

(b) The conduct of members of the Company in relation to one another, and to the Company and to the Company's servants.

(c) The setting aside of the whole or any part or parts of the Estate at any particular time or times or for a particular purpose or purposes.

(d) The procedure at general meetings and meetings of the directors and committees of the directors of the Company insofar as such procedure is not regulated by these Articles.

(e) And, generally, all such matters as are commonly the subject matter of company rules or rules or regulations appropriate to property of a similar nature and type as the Estate.

14.2 The Company in general meeting shall have power to alter or repeal the rules or bye-laws and to make additions thereto and the directors shall adopt such means as they deem sufficient to bring to the notice of members of the Company all such rules or bye-laws, which so long as they shall be in force, shall be binding on all members of the Company. Provided, nevertheless, that no rule or bye-law shall be inconsistent with, or shall affect or repeal anything contained in, the Memorandum or Articles of Association of the Company.

Form 15: Notice of AGM

NOTICE OF AGM

FLATCO LTD

Company number:

The Companies Act 1985

NOTICE is hereby given that the Annual General Meeting of Flatco Limited will be held at .... on .... [*date*] at ....am/pm to transact the business as shown on the attached Agenda including where appropriate the passing of ordinary resolutions as to the ordinary business of the Company (and to vote on any special resolutions detailed in the Agenda – if applicable).

By order of the Board   ....

Company Secretary

Date: ....

Notes:

1. Any member of the Company entitled to attend, speak and vote at the AGM may appoint a proxy to attend, speak and, on a poll, vote instead of that member. A proxy may demand, or join in demanding, a poll. A proxy need not be a member of the Company.

2. The instrument appointing a proxy must be deposited at the Registered Office of the company at least 48 hours prior to the AGM in order to be valid.

3. A copy of the balance sheet and every document required by law to be annexed to it, which are to be laid before the AGM are enclosed. The statutory registers may be inspected at any time upon request at the Registered Office of the company.

(Attach accounts and Agenda)

Form 16: AGM agenda

AGM AGENDA

Company number:

FLATCO LIMITED
ANNUAL GENERAL MEETING
AGENDA

1. Approval of notice convening meeting.
2. Approval of minutes of last AGM.
3. Matters arising.
4. Correspondence and communications.
5. Reports of directors.
6. Accounts.
7. Auditors.
8. Election of officers.
9. Consideration of budget.
10. Any other business.

By order of the Board

....

Company Secretary

Date ....

Form 17: AGM minutes

AGM MINUTES

Company number:

FLATCO LIMITED

Minutes of the Annual General Meeting of Flatco Limited held on

.... at ....

Present: (Here list those present entitled to vote)

_____

In attendance: (Here list anyone present but *not* entitled to vote)

- -

NOTICE OF MEETING: The company secretary confirmed that the notice convening the meeting had been sent to every member, the directors and the auditors and all others entitled to receive a copy of same. The notice convening the meeting was approved.

PREVIOUS MINUTES: The minutes of the preceding AGM were read and IT WAS RESOLVED that these be approved (subject to any amendments resulting from matters arising) and signed by the chairman as a true record.

CORRESPONDENCE AND COMMUNICATIONS: (Here detail any that may have been raised)

DIRECTORS' REPORTS: (Here detail any reports made)

ACCOUNTS: The annual accounts for the preceding year (including required reports) were laid before the meeting and the [Auditor's report]† was read, having been open to inspection during the meeting.

†AUDITORS: IT WAS RESOLVED subject to their agreement to reappoint Messrs .... as auditors of the company until the conclusion of the next Annual General Meeting.

ELECTIONS: (Here detail any elections that took place, eg if re-appointing directors retiring by rotation)

BUDGET: (Here detail discussions of the next year's budget and any resolutions that ensued)

OTHER BUSINESS: (Insert full details including type and text of all resolutions passed)

Form 17: AGM minutes

There being no further business the meeting was ended.

Signature:

....

Chairman of the meeting

                       Date ....

†Delete if audit exempt

Form 18: Model service charge account

MODEL SERVICE CHARGE ACCOUNT

FLATCO LIMITED

EXPENDITURE STATEMENT/SERVICE CHARGE DEMAND FOR
Y/E ....

PROPERTY:

SERVICE CHARGE EXPENDITURE:

(list as appropriate – likely items listed below)

1. Cleaning/Maintenance
2. Electricity/Heating
3. Staff
4. Gardens
5. Insurance
6. Audit Fees
7. Security
8. Miscellaneous

Total expenditure	£	
Proportion payable in respect of your property – %	£	
Less: money paid on account	(£	)
Balance due	£	
Add: (a) ground rent for coming year	£	
(b) reserve fund contribution (if extraordinary expenditure forecast)	£	
Total due	£	

[Insert full name and address of landlord]

Note: If paying by standing order, please revise your payments with effect
from .... to £ .... in accordance with the budget for next year.

[This is a simple form – professional assistance is advisable when the
property is large and involves major expenditure.]

Form 19: Letter to flat-owners enclosing service charge/year end accounts

LETTER TO FLAT OWNERS

[Use headed paper from management company]

Date:

To: All Flat-owners
    xxxxxxxxxx
    xxxxxxxxx

Dear Flat-owner

We have now finalised this year's accounts and the audited accounts are enclosed/are available for inspection by you.

We now enclose a service charge demand for last year's expenditure showing how much is now due from you/to your credit. If an amount is owing, can you let us have a cheque as soon as possible. If a credit is shown, this will be carried forward/a refund in your favour is enclosed. We have kept as close to the original estimate as possible but the additional expenditure is as a result of .... [*insert reasons*]

Next year's estimate is also enclosed. No extraordinary expenditure is anticipated/Please note the provision for decorating the exterior which this year results in a higher than average estimate.

We also attach details of the property insurance renewal (attach if required)

If you have any queries plase contact the Company Secretary.

Yours sincerely

Director/Company Secretary

Appendix **Two**
Useful Addresses

Citizens' Advice Bureaux
- see under Citizens' Advice Bureau in your local telephone directory

Companies House
Crown Way
Cardiff
CF14 3UZ
Tel: 02920 388588

Companies House
102 George Street
Edinburgh
EH2 3DJ
Tel: 0131 225 5774

Incorporated Society of Valuers & Auctioneers
3 Cadogan Gate
London
SW1X 0AS
Tel: 0207 235 2282

Inland Revenue
- see under Inland Revenue in your local telephone directory

Institute of Chartered Secretaries & Administrators
16 Park Crescent
London
W1N 4AH
Tel: 0207 580 4741

Royal Institution of Chartered Surveyors
12 Great George Street
London
SW1P 3AD
Tel: 0207 222 7000

VAT
- see under HM Customs and Excise in your local telephone directory

Index

References are to page numbers

Service charges - *cont*
  clause in lease, form of   53–4
  collection by management
     company   63, 87–8, 118
  estimate   63, 183
    accountants, use for   124
    management accounts
      assist   90
  letter to flat-owners with   184
  obligation   52, 53–4
  standing order, payment by
    63
Services   2
Share capital   10, 18
  see also Shares
  annual return, details in   111
  reference on letter, etc, to
    113
Share certificate, *see* Shares
Share company   10–11
  authorised and issued capital
    10, 18
  liability, *see* Limited liability
  membership, *see* Member
    (company)
  shares, *see* Shares
Shareholder, *see* Meeting, general;
  Member (company)
Shares
  allotment and issue   11, 67,
    97
    notification, filing return
      99, 100, 131
    procedure check-list   100
    register of applications and
      allotment   107
  certificates   67, 97, 100
    blank   107
    cancellation of old   100
    new   100
    sealing   100
  directors' interests, register
    67–8, 107, 108
  payment   11, 100

  transfer   11–12, 67, 98, 100,
    102–3
    form   100, 132
    membership register, noted
      in   100
    register of   107–8
    stamp duty   102
  value   11, 12
Sinking fund   22, 55, 62, 87
  meaning   62
Small block   11, 26–7, 49, 71,
    75
  accountants, use of   124, 125
  expenditure for   88
  two flats
    minimum   28, 40
    only   1, 2–3
Solicitor
  enfranchisement, for   25, 27,
    28, 30, 37
  fees   16, 21, 123
  formation, for   14, 125
  freehold purchase, of   19–21,
    125
    costs   16
  lease, advice on   19–20, 22,
    56, 126
  statutory registers,
    preparation   126
  transfer of membership, for
    102
Staircase   55, 61
Stamp duty   16, 21
  share transfer form   102
Stationery   16
  company name on   112–13
  failure   112
  details on   112–13
  directors   113
Statutory accounts, *see* Accounts,
  annual (statutory)
Statutory books   65, 66–7,
  106–9
  see also specific registers